"What a gem of a book! In a crowded world run of self-help books, this is the one everyone should have on their shelf. Kris is living proof that her simple yet effective energy healing practices can help us become the best and healthiest versions of ourselves. This is a fun and practical guidebook that everyone can benefit from."

—Amy B. Scher, bestselling author of *How to Heal Yourself from Anxiety When No One Else Can*

"Kris Ferraro's new book, *Energy Healing* is a true gift! She leads the reader through an understanding of what energy is, how it works in the body, and how to heal a myriad of issues in your life with simple, easy-to-follow practices. Hers is a voice of compassion, encouragement, joy, and wonder. I can't think of a better guide through this field. The book is full of wonderful and simple ways to get your energy working for you, and why it matters. You couldn't find a better way to start or deepen your understanding of energy than to pick up this book."

—Lauren Walker, international yoga teacher, creator of EMYoga, author of *Energy Medicine Yoga* and *The Energy Medicine Yoga Prescription*.

"We are in an era where people are taking more control of their health and decisions about recovery and healing. Never has it been easier to access knowledge and information, and of course evidence. Kris's book offers a practical guide to a growing area in complementary approaches and provides actual tools you can start using right now. There is a 4th wave of therapy approaches emerging and they are body based—this book outlines how these methods can be used to reduce, relieve, and address stress in the body and let's be honest: most people are looking for that. Enjoy the read and the application—this is undoubtedly the future of the therapy space."

—Dr. Peta Stapleton, associate professor, Bond University (Australia) and author of *The Science Behind Tapping: A Proven Stress Management Technique for the Mind and Body*

"Kris Ferraro has given us a most helpful book for those interested in learning about energy healing. She presents the theory and practices in a way that newcomers to the field can easily benefit, for it is one of the most comprehensive and easy-to-use guides for beginners I have seen. I highly recommend it."

—Henry Grayson, Ph.D., author of *Your Power to Heal*

"*Energy Healing: The Start Here Guide for Beginners* is a comprehensive resource for living a balanced, hopeful, and empowered life. It offers clear, honest, and functional ways to understand, develop, and integrate energy healing practices into daily life, whether that means getting out of bed feeling good, grounding and calming the nervous system, coming to terms with troubles and trauma, or opening more fully to life's possibilities. Kris's own heartfelt life stories of triumph didn't come overnight, and that only deepens the authenticity and authority of the book's offerings. *Energy Healing* is like a wise and gentle friend who "gets" you, and who shares nuggets on how to keep returning to yourself, again and again over the years. Enjoy this treasure!"

—Kathilyn Solomon, EFT tapping coach and teacher and author of *Tapping into Wellness: Using EFT to Clear Emotional and Physical Pain and Illness*

"Kris Ferraro takes a concept that might seem out of reach and complicated and makes it not only accessible, but fun to practice (and the
book is full of practices . . . you will find at least one that works for
you). She approaches her subject with professionalism, empathy, and
humor. Kris is a gifted teacher—let her show you the way!"
—Karen C.L. Anderson, writer, master-certified life coach, and author of *Difficult Mothers, Adult Daughters: A Guide For Separation,
Liberation and Inspiration*

"Boom! This one rocks. *Energy Healing* is completely satisfying. It's at
once an easy-to-understand how-to, and a very personal and relatable
story most everyone can resonate with, about how most of us eventually
come to energy work. Not by any means least, this book is like a warm,
funny, conversation with a friend who's sharing something cool and
helpful. Kris Ferraro's signature style is intrinsically like that—in this
first (of many I am sure) works that speak to the human condition, she
finds organic ways to make us smile in self-reflection, understand we're
not alone, and like a flashlight of saving grace, point the way through
the dark times. You are guaranteed to enjoy this book, and even if
you're a seasoned energy fan, you'll find several things you didn't know.
This is the whole package for beginning to understand what energy
healing, medicine, and psychology are all about, and how to start using
them for yourself. Brava!"
—Jondi Whitis, master trainer of trainers for EFT International
and author of *How to Be a Great Detective: The Handy-Dandy Guide to
Using Kindness, Compassion and Curiosity to Resolve Emotional, Mental
and Physical Upsets—For Tappers, Practitioners and Caregivers*

"I wish I had this book when I was struggling to make sense of this
world as a highly sensitive twenty-three-year-old and my life was an
unmanageable hot mess! Kris takes concepts that took me years to
master and makes them readily accessible. She breaks everything
down with clear, concise explanations and then offers simple DOABLE

actions so anyone with a few minutes of time and willingness to experiment can try them.

Even after more than three decades exploring many forms of energy healing, I still found valuable gems on nearly every page. Kris breathes new life into some of my go-to techniques, providing a fresh perspective for this seasoned professional. Whether you are just considering this book as a possible next step on your path, or are an experienced practitioner, *Energy Healing* will be a must-have resource guide for your library.

Don't be fooled by the brevity of this volume. Kris delivers information with a precision that distills each topic and tool to its purest form. I have no doubt my copy will become a dog-eared favorite and a frequent gift for my clients and loved ones."

—Jennifer Elizabeth Moore, EFT master trainer and author of *Empathic Mastery*

"What a treat this book is! After providing the reader with a thorough yet practical introduction to the basics of Energy Healing, Kris then takes us on a journey of the benefits of putting this information to use. She lays out easy, step-by-step methods to practice a variety of energy-optimizing tools, providing options for customizing to suit individual needs. Kris's book provides a much-needed resource to shed light on these practices. She even puts it all together to give a great example of how to incorporate the techniques into daily life. Read this book and begin your Energy Healing journey today."

— Terry Maluk, author of *Rx for RNs: A Step-by-Step Guide to Manage Stress, Reduce Overwhelm, and Conquer Burnout.*

ENERGY
HEALING

••••

SIMPLE AND EFFECTIVE PRACTICES
TO BECOME YOUR OWN HEALER

{ A Start Here Guide }

KRIS FERRARO

ST. MARTIN'S
ESSENTIALS
New York

The information in this book is not intended to replace the advice of the reader's own physician or other medical professional. You should consult a medical professional in matters relating to health, especially if you have existing medical conditions, and before starting, stopping, or changing the dose of any medication you are taking. Individual readers are solely responsible for their own health-care decisions. The author and the publisher do not accept responsibility for any adverse effects individuals may claim to experience, whether directly or indirectly, from the information contained in this book.

The fact that an organization or website is mentioned in the book as a potential source of information does not mean that the author or the publisher endorses any of the information they may provide or recommendations they may make.

The stories in this book are composite, fictional accounts based on the experiences of many individuals. Similarities to any real person or persons are coincidental and unintentional.

For my Mom, Betty Maloney Ferraro

CONTENTS

INTRODUCTION

Perhaps you've picked up this book out of curiosity. More and more people seem to be exploring different ways to release stress, get relaxed, silence pain, and feel better. "Maybe there is something to this stuff," you're thinking.

Or perhaps you've picked up this book because you are experiencing emotional or physical pain. The stress is weighing more heavily than it has before. You don't remember the last time you truly felt at ease, aggravated by racing, anxious thoughts or being on high alert. Or you have annoying physical symptoms that don't seem to go away no matter what you've tried. You suspect you're not digesting your food properly. Or you get every cold or flu that comes along. "There has to be a better way," you're thinking. "Maybe this will help."

I'd like to welcome you to relief. And relief using your very own hands and body!

I'd like to welcome you to "new" ways of healing, many of which are actually ancient ways of healing. Most have just gotten lost in modern life and are now being revived for a new audience. Some have used ancient elements, like energy meridians (or pathways), to form new practices with a modern bent.

In this guide you will learn what energy is, which widely known modalities are available, and how you can get your energy working for you. I've included tips on being both safe and effective along with ways to get your energy moving in the correct direction. You'll start neutralizing your uncomfortable emotions using Emotional Freedom Techniques (EFT), so you are no longer at the mercy of your upset. These simple practices can make you feel calmer, happier, healthier, and much more in tune with yourself than you've been before.

I'm incredibly honored to be sharing this life-changing information with you. Because this information has radically changed every area of my life.

I've been on a perpetual search for as long as I can remember. There was a small voice inside me that told me I could live a life without constant fear and finally be happy. In the mid-'90s, I began working as a counselor in a social service agency, helping people in the traditional ways: listening, providing resources, educating, making opportunities, and fulfilling immediate needs. Outside of my traditional 9-to-5, I began studying hypnotherapy. I noticed that my clients often seemed stuck in unhealthy mental loops, which negatively affected how they saw themselves. I believed that life could be different for them, but most of the time, they just could not believe that themselves. Studying the subconscious mind gave me answers for how these loops were created. Then my hypnotherapy teacher introduced me to EFT as we tapped on my romantic woes. We talked, I wept, and we tapped about it all. It was only a couple years later that I realized that the pattern had been healed. I knew I had to study this weird tapping thing! So, sixteen years ago I began doing just that, taking live classes and studying every article, video, and interview I could find. I just devoured it all. Here was what I had been looking for. The answer to my overwhelming feelings of fear. The answer to releasing all the emotional baggage I had been dragging around. I learned my sensitivity made me able to feel energy shifts. This aspect of my personality that I blamed for my pain was actually a gift, and one that lended itself well to this work. EFT opened a new world of other energy principles and practices to me. When I wasn't working, I was studying and practicing, until that *became* my work. For ten years now, I have helped my clients heal using EFT and other energy-shifting modalities. From neutralizing a bad memory to ending regular panic attacks to releasing life-limiting patterns, I have the best career in the world. I get to facilitate "miracles" for a living. Because when you know how to change your energy, your entire world changes, from the inside out. And those changes can seem miraculous, although not rare or seemingly random as miracles are often thought of. I get to speak to and teach thousands of people about some of the very principles and practices I'm now sharing in this book. I wake up every day excited to share what I know.

This book is filled with practical, easy, step-by-step processes to get you working with your own energy fast. I encourage you to try everything and see how you feel. Then continue working with what works well for you.

Let this guide get you into deeper connection with your own energy, emotions, and intuition. Some profound changes can come from learning to listen to what your pain is trying to tell you. Then allow that connection to be your companion as you practice. Always work *with* and not *against* your body, so don't do anything that feels painful. When learning any healing modalities, use good judgment and common sense. It's natural to want to dive right in and start transforming already! But there are many times a gentle approach, like learning and practicing a bit daily, reaps greater benefits. And please know that working with a qualified healing professional is always an option and sometimes it is the best one. I've included a chapter on when to seek outside help along with tips for finding the ideal practitioner for you.

PART I

••••

ENERGY HEALING

WHAT IS ENERGY?

The word *energy* invokes a few different ideas. From the physical energy of the body, and how that may be lagging, to the energy crisis and what to do about it, this common word is a bit of a mystery, even in scientific circles. Physics textbooks define energy as "the capacity to do work." So, the definition itself is what it *does*, not what it actually *is*. From the perspective of the physicist, energy is either conserved or converted into mass, otherwise known as form.

But I'm not a scientist. I'm a healer. I view energy as the composition of life. When I learned how to listen to, and work with, my own energy, I became the master of my life. That's what I want for you. To get you started, I'm sharing simple, practical, and effective practices to enable you to become your own healer.

And you may be interested to know that there *are* numerous scientific studies on energy healing modalities like EFT. They demonstrate what healers throughout time have always known: this stuff *works*.

MY SIMPLE OVERVIEW OF WHAT ENERGY IS

Energy is the very essence of life itself. Absolutely *everything* is made up of energy. The very atoms that compose all life are made of invisible energy. Whether you are sitting on a chair, a patch of grass, a concrete slab, or a sandy beach as you read this, you are sitting on energy. Every person, including you, is a unique ordering of energy. It takes form in what appears solid, like your bones, skin, and teeth. It's also the building blocks of seemingly intangible qualities like your sense of humor, fear of dogs, and love of the color purple. It is the soil, rocks, water, and fire that make up the earth. It's the invisible atmosphere surrounding every planet and star. And it's the planets and stars themselves. It's the internal force that causes the flowers to bloom each spring, right on time. It's the external force that brings the tides in and sends them back out. It's the ocean water and all it comprises: hydrogen, oxygen, salt, minutiae of seaweed, sediment, and fish scales. Energy is what happens when sperm meets egg and a new human is formed, one cell division at a time. Yes, it does indeed have the capacity to do the work. And in fact, it's the only force that can.

You may have noticed I said, "It takes form in what appears solid." That's an important piece to ponder. Although the foundation of your home may feel quite solid—after all, it's holding up an entire building—the truth is, *nothing* is actually solid.

Matter is moving particles, and the form they take can be denser, like a house or a bone, or looser, like a thought or a feeling. But all particles are in a state of movement.

Particles are made up of subatomic particles. It was believed that particles could never be split, but science has now shown they can indeed be split; they just no longer hold the information for that substance. If you have a particle of copper and a particle of lead, those particles are the smallest pieces of those elements. If you split both of these particles into subatomic particles, they will no longer resemble copper or lead. Those subatomic particles will look identical to each other. They're like anonymous substances that are able to take form as anything and everything. This is what I think of when I think of energy.

Again, this is a very simplified overview of energy. I won't be looking for my Nobel Prize in physics. Not this year, anyway!

I have a point in sharing this. If you're working with energy, then know you are working with this anonymous substance that makes up all of life. All of it! Everything that *is* you and everything that is *outside* of you. Everything that is *everything*. You may have heard popular statements like "We are all connected" or "We are all one." That's what those statements mean to me. Of course, we are all connected, because we are all made up of the same stuff! That stuff is energy.

When you work with the very substance of life, endless possibilities to heal are now available to you.

EXPERIENCING ENERGY HEALING

But the truth is, as fascinating as theory is, it's not my focus. Energy healing can be read about, researched, theorized, plotted, hypothesized, and studied. But you will only understand its power once you actually feel it, work with it, and experience it for yourself.

I'm an Energy Coach. If you're wondering what that is, well, you'd be asking the same question my family has for the last ten years! I work with clients who want to change something in their lives that's holding them back. Maybe they haven't felt like themselves since a parent died many years before. Or they feel constantly overwhelmed by even the small aspects of daily living. Or the stress of work or family has become unmanageable. Or, even though they are intelligent, good people, they feel badly about themselves. They know this is having a negative impact on their lives but don't know why they feel this way or how to change it. Often, they've tried to make positive life changes but can't seem to make much progress. By the time they've arrived in my practice, they've tried just about everything else and haven't found much relief. I begin an energetic investigation. No magic wands necessary. I speak with them about how they feel, finding blocked areas causing or containing their symptoms (grief, overwhelm, low self-esteem, a memory, or belief), and direct the flow of energy to liberate those feelings or patterns. All without touching them in any way. I don't possess any special powers. I wasn't born with second sight. There's actually nothing esoteric or "woo woo" about this work. The results may seem magical indeed. But it's not magic; it's energy in motion!

I'm here to leave out the "woo woo" and make energy healing practical, easy to understand, and doable. I have a strong left brain at work in my noggin, so anything too cryptic and mysterious is lost on me completely. There's no need for mystery anyway. Energy healing is natural. Modern life may have become detached from it, but it's simple enough to integrate it back in again. That's what we will be doing together.

Some Basic Energy Principles to Keep in Mind

- **Your energy enters a room before you do.** Your energy is silently communicating with the energy of the people you interact with, and you may be mostly unaware of this. Normally your attention will become conscious of it when it's intense. Have you ever just somehow *known* a person was angry with you, even when all outside appearances seemed normal? She smiles and shakes your hand, but you just *know* there's a problem? Or walked into a room where, unbeknownst to you, an argument had taken place and it just felt "off" or uncomfortable? You were reading the energy in those situations.

- **Energy is designed to flow.** It just needs space to do it. Think of a cluttered room. When I enter a disorderly room, my energy feels heavy and weighted down. It makes sense because energy is not moving as freely in that space as it could. Remove the clutter and flow is reestablished. This is why people report miraculous shifts after doing a thorough shedding of unneeded items. They might get a raise or meet a new partner or lose weight. The energy in their space is flowing and so is the energy in the other areas of their lives. When you think of energy, equate flow with feeling good.

From an energetic perspective, all problems are caused by congestion and all healing or relief comes from flow. If you put in a dam to stop a fast-moving river, as the water becomes still, mold will begin to form. In fact, mold can only form in water in which there is no movement. A repeated emotional outburst, a tumor in the body, and a lacking financial pattern are investigated the same way. Where has energy gotten stuck? How did it get stagnant? And how can it start flowing again?

WHAT IS ENERGY HEALING?

My focus is on healing. Or call it relief, change, transformation, progress, growth. Whether it's my life or the lives of my clients, my focus is on what can be done to correct a problematic condition. For the most part, I'm not overly concerned with *how* this stuff works, just that it does indeed *work*. I'm not waiting for anyone to come along and prove what I already know to be true. I do remain grateful for my colleagues who are out in the world of academia, conducting studies that are showing compelling results. And even though I'm not a scientist, I do approach healing somewhat like one. My life and the lives of my loved ones, colleagues, clients, and students are my laboratory. When studying how a healing energy practice works in "a lab," I document the problem and then detail what was used and how it was applied, what was uncovered or learned, and, finally, the results. Which practices were most effective? Can the same results be achieved with less time and/or effort? Which practices didn't seem to work or didn't work well enough? What could have been done instead or in addition to? How did the client resonate with the modality or practice? As for results, I test, test, and test again. I'm not satisfied with modest results. I want outstanding ones.

What I offer in this book are principles and practices I've worked with over and over again. They've been proven to be safe, highly effective, easy to learn, and appropriate for beginners.

Energy healing comprises multiple practices that have been done in every culture, all over the globe, for thousands of years. I'm sure many of these practices never received a title or had books written about them. They were just a part of everyday life in those cultures during those times. Children were raised doing them. People did them in public. Practices were passed down within families, generation after generation. Everybody did them, so nothing was considered weird or strange. Various forms of energy healing were just normal. After all, in the days before antibiotics, X-rays, and therapy, people were limited. Being able to heal oneself and one another was a biological necessity. Only healthy people could advance civilization forward.

Modern society has gifted us with the most incredible advances in the areas of medicine and technology. It can be easy to get distracted and disconnected from nature itself and from our own true nature. But we don't have to live in an either/or world. We can work with our own innate energy, bringing balance to our bodies and minds, *and* take full advantage of modern advances when useful. What an amazing time we live in!

{ 3 }

ENERGY HEALING MODALITIES

There are hundreds, if not thousands, of different energy healing modalities. I've included some brief information on a few of the better known and more widely practiced ones here. This can give you a sense of the broad ingenuity that has created multiple methods for providing comfort and relief. If interested in professional sessions with a healer or practitioner, this can also help you decide which modality may be best for your specific needs.

Note: I've included a Resources section in the back with places to find more information.

Each modality has some general guidelines for easy comparison. For each modality I write about here, I include:

- **Effective For:** Most energy healing modalities are thought to help a wide range of physical, mental, and emotional conditions. From allergies to anxiety, stage fright to sciatica, insomnia to immunity concerns, there is likely someone, somewhere, who believes that an energy healing technique improved that condition. In fact, I'm sure there are many someones who feel that way. When a modality is widely known to be effective for a particular condition, I have included it here.

- **Important Note:** Energy healers do not "treat" conditions, as medical professionals do. We approach both physical and emotional symptoms the same way, as energetic imbalances. We search for areas of congestion (or blockages) and use various methods to release these blockages, allowing energy to flow more freely. It is believed a body that has free-flowing energy can heal itself. This free-flowing energy can provide great relief, improving painful conditions of all kinds.

- **Session Types:** There are various ways to work with energy healers, so I've included a description of different types here.

  IN PERSON: You meet with the healer in his/her office, your home, or another agreed-upon location.

  REMOTE: Can be done online, using video conferencing with Skype or Zoom, where healer and client can see each other. Or you can communicate the old-fashioned way (by phone).

  SURROGATE: The healer tunes in to your energy field and creates shifts without you being present, whether in-person or remotely. Often this comes with a follow-up phone call or email with the healer's findings.

- **Body Position:** If you're working with a healer in person, it can be helpful to know if you will be lying down on a massage table or sitting upright in a chair, and whether you stay fully clothed or need to undress for treatment.

- **Physical Touch:** Does the healer make direct contact with the physical body? You may be interested to learn that most modalities do not. Some place their hands around the body and others don't come into close physical contact at all.

   Note: To legally touch a client, a healer must ask the client for consent (permission) and have a massage license or be a medical professional or clergy member, like a minister. Or the modality itself includes a license for touch, as it is with acupuncture. Laws about this vary by state. Check your state's laws. When hiring a healing professional, I strongly encourage you to ask if physical touch is used. If so, clearly express where and how you want to be touched and not touched. Ask what license they have that allows them to legally touch clients.

> **Energy, chi, ki, qi, and prana are all terms that mean the same thing. They refer to the life force and vitality in all beings.**

MODALITIES
Acupuncture/Acupressure

Effective For: A wide variety of physical and emotional health challenges; found to be very effective for pain relief.

Session Type: In-person only. Some insurance companies cover cost for acupuncture treatments, usually for treatment of pain.

Body Position: Lying down, without socks. Partial disrobement, like pant legs rolled up or shirt pulled up to expose back or stomach, is often needed.

Physical Touch: Yes. Acupuncturists place thin needles in the body. Acupressure is done with direct touch on the body.

Practiced in the East for thousands of years, acupuncture is part of a comprehensive health system called Traditional Chinese Medicine. For thousands of years, the Chinese have known of pathways or channels of energy called meridians. Acupuncture works by inserting tiny needles into these pathways to bring balance to the energy system. Acupressure does the same, but without needles. Hands are placed in specific areas along the meridian pathways to release energy blocks and establish balance.

Brennan Healing Science/Brennan Integration Work

Effective For: A wide variety of physical, mental-emotional health, and spiritual challenges

Session Type: In-person, remote

Body Position: Lying down or sitting, fully clothed

Physical Touch: For hands-on healings, hands are placed lightly on the body or in the energetic field around the body.

After years of researching and studying numerous healing modalities, Barbara Brennan developed Brennan Healing Science (BHS), a holistic healing modality based on the Human Energy-Consciousness System and its relationship to health and disease. Barbara saw a human being as existing in four dimensions. The main dimension is the dimension where we can feel our divinity and oneness with all beings. The physical body arises out of the energy field. An imbalance or blockage in this field will eventually cause a disease in the physical body. Therefore, healing blockages in the energy field will bring about healing in the physical body.

Cranial Sacral Therapy and Massage

Effective For: A wide variety of physical and emotional health challenges

Session Type: In-person

Body Position: Lying on a massage table, clothed

Physical Touch: Yes

Practitioners use soft touch on parts of the head, neck, and ears to create balance in the cranial sacral system and central nervous system. Believed to alleviate tensions in the brain and spinal column, thereby creating greater flow, it was created by osteopathic physician John E. Upledger after extensive testing and research. Not advisable for people with an aneurysm or cerebral hemorrhage as this method increases blood flow in the brain.

Emotional Freedom Techniques (EFT or Tapping)

(See Chapter 8, page 95)

Effective For: A wide variety of physical and emotional health challenges

Session Type: In-person, remote, and sometimes surrogate

Body Position: Sitting

Physical Touch: Mostly none. While there are a few practitioners who tap on their clients, the majority do not. The practitioner taps on him- or herself while leading the client in self tapping. Often the client mirrors the practitioner's tapping.

Stanford-educated engineer Gary Craig developed EFT after having trained in Thought Field Therapy (TFT), created by the late Dr. Roger Callahan. Gary Craig saw the potential in streamlining complicated algorithms used in the process while maintaining effectiveness. He created one recipe that included most of the main meridians and encouraged early adopters to "try it on everything." A practitioner helps the client to release stress by allowing specific painful events from the past to become conscious and then gently neutralized, through tapping on meridian points.

Emotion Code/Body Code

Effective For: A wide variety of physical and emotional health challenges

Session Type: In-person, remote, and surrogate

Body Position: Any

Physical Touch: Usually none. The muscle testing for some in-person sessions may include gently pressing down on a client's wrist while an arm is raised.

A system created by chiropractor Dr. Bradley Nelson, where the healer uses muscle testing to identify places of energy blockage on charts (see page 64 for more information on this), Emotion Code uses a chart of trapped emotions. Once identified, they are released using a magnet. With in-person sessions, the magnet is run down the client's spine from the shoulders to the tailbone. The magnet does not need to touch the body. For remote or surrogate sessions, the client will run the magnet themselves, starting between the eyebrows, going up and over the top of the head and down the middle of the back of the head. Emotion Code can be done alone or as part of a larger system called Body Code, which includes a series of charts, called Mind Maps, to identify blockages and misalignment in several areas.

Energy Clearing (from Jean Haner)

The term "energy clearing" can be used to describe different practices. This description is specifically about the method created by Jean Haner.

Effective For: A wide variety of physical and emotional health challenges

Session Type: In-person, remote, and surrogate

Body Position: Sitting upright, fully clothed

Physical Touch: No

This type of energy-clearing process uses a pendulum and a dowsing rod to clear the energy of people and spaces. The practitioner gets into a passive wondering state, without a specific agenda for results, and clears eight different energy levels, including the Five Elements from Traditional Chinese Medicine. A practitioner or client may experience releases that are happening and information about what is being cleared, but not always. Changes are most often experienced after several short sessions.

Energy Medicine (Eden Energy Medicine from Donna Eden and Dr. David Feinstein)

The term "energy medicine" can be used to describe different practices. This description is specifically about Eden Energy Medicine, as created by energy healing pioneer Donna Eden.

Effective For: A wide variety of physical and emotional health challenges

Session Type: Mainly in person

Body Position: Usually lying down, fully clothed

Physical Touch: Yes. The practitioner uses several different energy-testing methods to make an assessment of the client. For example, the client may be asked to raise an arm while the practitioner presses on it for testing. Practitioners may press into meridian pathways or massage points, or sweep their hands over the body.

Eden Energy Medicine uses energy testing (more detailed assessments than muscle testing) to assess nine energy systems of the body, including the meridians and chakras, so practices can be administered to bring flow and balance to these systems. Donna Eden actually sees energy. She was able to create a comprehensive system that boosts the immune system and brings clarity, productivity, and vitality. Practitioners do thorough assessments of Five Elements theory and perform several practices to restore balance.

Healing Touch

Effective For: A wide variety of physical and emotional health challenges. Well known to successfully speed healing in postoperative recovery.

Session Type: In-person

Body Position: Usually lying fully clothed on a massage table

Physical Touch: Yes

Created and practiced by licensed nurses, this modality is unique in that it is often administered in hospitals and other medical settings. The nurses use light touch to create energetic flow in all areas of the body. Healing Touch has been researched and found to be helpful in healing many physical ailments. Patients also rate treatments highly effective. It is found where integrative medicine is practiced.

Jin Shin Jyutsu®

Effective For: A wide variety of physical and emotional health challenges

Session Type: In-person

Body Position: Usually lying fully clothed on a massage table

Physical Touch: Yes

This practice is believed to have been passed down as a tradition through generations in Japan. It was almost lost until a man named Master Jiro Murai used it to heal himself and then shared the technique in the early 1900s. Practitioners hold certain places on the body to reduce energy blockages and increase the movement of energy (or chi) throughout the body.

Pranic Healing

Effective For: A wide variety of physical and emotional health challenges

Session Type: In-person

Body Position: Usually sitting or lying down, fully clothed

Physical Touch: No. Practitioners move energy outside of the body.

Pranic Healing was created and developed by Master Choa Kok Sui as a method for cleansing the body's energy field and increasing the flow of prana (energy). Practitioners feel for areas of "dirty" energy, cleanse with movements in the auric field, and sometimes use liquid sprays designed for energy clearing. They then strengthen the prana, enabling the body to heal itself.

Reiki

Effective For: A wide variety of physical and emotional health challenges

Session Type: In-person, remote, and surrogate

Body Position: Lying down or sitting, fully clothed

Physical Touch: Mostly no. Hands are placed around the outside of the body without manual touch. In some exceptions, a practitioner will administer light touch on the head, hands, or feet.

Created in Japan, Reiki creates healing by reducing stress and enhancing deep relaxation. The Japanese word for energy or life force is *ki*. If your ki is low, then you are more susceptible to ailments. Reiki increases this life force energy so that ailments can dissipate. A Reiki practitioner works in the auric field to increase energy flow. Most clients report feeling relaxed and peaceful.

Rubenfeld Synergy Method

Effective For: A wide variety of physical and emotional health challenges

Session Type: In-person

Body Position: Lying on a massage table, clothed

Physical Touch: Yes, light touch

Created by Ilana Rubenfeld out of her training in the Alexander Technique, a method for improving posture and everyday movements for pain relief, this modality combines bodywork, intuition, and psychotherapy. Practitioners feel for areas of blockage, bringing their hands to those locations. They then dialogue with the client, asking questions about their problems and inviting information forward from the subconscious mind, allowing emotions to be released and clarity to be achieved.

Shiatsu Massage

Effective For: A wide variety of physical and emotional health challenges

Session Type: In-person

Body Position: Lying on a massage table, mostly clothed

Physical Touch: Yes

From Japan, shiatsu (she-ott-sue) uses the meridians from Traditional Chinese Medicine to release blockages and create flow. Pressure is applied using the fingers, hands, and elbows. The massage may also involve actively rotating the joints. It's known to improve the circulation system as well as stiff muscles. Like all meridian-based modalities, healing can affect all levels of physical and emotional well-being.

Tai Chi and Qigong

Effective For: A wide variety of physical and emotional health challenges

Session Type: Learn from large or small in-person classes, private instruction, online videos, DVDs, or books.

Body Position: You move while standing upright.

Physical Touch: Instructors normally don't touch students.

Part of Traditional Chinese Medicine, tai chi (tie-chee) and qigong (chee-gong) are eastern forms of exercise that promote the flow of chi (energy) in the body. The movements are slow, conscious, and fluid. They can be very gentle or a bit more challenging, depending on each person's stamina and flexibility. Appropriate for all ages and health levels, many seniors enjoy the increased balance and well-being a practice provides. In the east, these modalities are practiced outside, connecting with nature, where groups do the movements in unison. Tai chi is considered a martial art while qigong is focused on healing. The movements for these two systems are different and it is believed that tai chi is one form of qigong.

ThetaHealing®

Effective For: A wide variety of physical and emotional health challenges

Session Type: In-person and remote

Body Position: Sitting, fully clothed

Physical Touch: None. Practitioners use a series of statements to do the clearing.

A form of energy healing that comes from a spiritual belief system, this modality encourages an uncovering of negative beliefs and their origins. The shifts are reported to happen instantaneously through the Creator.

Thought Field Therapy (TFT)

Effective For: A wide variety of physical and emotional health challenges

Session Type: In person and remote

Body Position: Sitting, fully clothed

Physical Touch: Mostly none. While there are a few practitioners who tap on their clients, most do not. The practitioner taps on him- or herself, while leading the client in self-tapping. Often the client mirrors the practitioner's tapping.

Dr. Roger Callahan was inspired to tap on certain meridian points while a patient described her crippling water phobia. Her phobia disappeared and hasn't returned decades later. Callahan knew he was on to something, and developed a series of protocols for a variety of emotional and physical conditions. Tapping on certain meridians in a specific order, these "recipes," called algorithms, were found to provide great relief.

{ 4 }

HOW ENERGY HEALING CAN CHANGE YOUR LIFE

Imagine getting into the ocean during high tide. The force of waves is pushing forward, bringing sand, shells, and debris with it. Then there's a momentary receding before it begins again, thrusting with a force that seems innocent on the shore, but menacing once you are immersed in it. You begin to understand how water carved out the Grand Canyon and the Valley of Fire. You dive under the waves but you can still feel the weight of the water pushing back. Finally, you get past where the waves are breaking, yet the rhythm of the tides is still there. You tread vigorously to stay in place but when you glance toward the lifeguard booth, you see you have somehow moved far past it. When you're ready to reach land once again, the water carries you back in, and in a fraction of the time and effort it took to get out there.

Now imagine a gently rolling river that is moving downstream. You settle into a canoe, sit back and are happy to find there's no need to paddle. You are moved forward with very little effort. The water carries you and does all the work. You allow yourself to be supported. Then the canoe gets stuck on a stubborn branch. You have plenty of energy to push off it and quickly begin moving downstream once again. The journey is gentle and relaxing.

In the first example, this is what daily living feels like when your energy is unbalanced and out of alignment. Every movement, every task, every change requires great effort, and sometimes that effort doesn't get you very far. There's a constant feeling of "moving against." You drink more coffee or eat a cupcake, craving that "quick hit" that will get you moving again. But the boost from stimulants feels chaotic or jittery and is followed by a crash. *Now* you're really tired. Life. Is. Hard.

The second example is what it feels like when you are moving with the flow of energy. Relaxed. Supported. In acceptance. Everything falling into place. The effort you exert meets the target and accomplishes the goal.

When I ask what energy healing can do for you, it's important I share what energy healing has done for me. You can see from my story that it can change everything.

HOW ENERGY HEALING HEALED ME

As I mature into my work as an Energy Coach, I can look back on different periods of my life and reevaluate them from an energetic perspective.

Every school has at least one kid who seems to be wearing an invisible Kick Me sign. (Which then attracts actual Kick Me signs!) This is the kid who gets bullied, gossiped about, and pushed around. If you take that kid out of their school and put him or her in another, often the cycle will just repeat itself. And when they grow up, they may enter careers and relationships where they are intimidated and manipulated. It would be natural to assume it's the child's appearance or another physical marker that's inviting this attention. But what I've found is that child is putting out an energetic signal that reads as fear and victimization. The energy of the other children tunes into this and then responds to it. How do I know that? Because I *was* that kid.

Having been bullied from kindergarten through high school wasn't a complete mystery. I had always just felt different. (It stopped in senior year only because people were scared of me by then. I had a foot-long Mohawk haircut, lots of black eyeliner, and a studded leather jacket. In the Bible Belt, this is a highly effective "shield.") Even during those rare time periods when my outside appearance seemed normal enough, it was still like I was sending out a signal, alerting bullies to my vulnerable presence.

I now know the other children were reading my crippling fear. I had always been a sensitive child. And many sensitive children grow up in insensitive environments that simply don't recognize it. This was true for me. By grade school, I had already started developing a serious anxiety disorder. For fourth grade, I was moved to a special school for "smart kids." I hadn't wanted to switch schools. All that change, with a new bus and new peers, just felt completely overwhelming and terrifying for me. But my parents wanted me to have the best education possible and, concerned I'd grow bored or not explore my full potential, they sent me off to what felt like a brand new world. Many of the educational materials in my new class were one, two, or three grade levels above my age. I had attention deficit disorder and an auditory processing disorder that had not been diagnosed. Many learning disabilities just weren't known at that time. I began to fall behind in my schoolwork and spent endless nights lying awake, paralyzed with fear. Never the athlete, schoolwork had always come easily to me. Now I was struggling with the one thing that made me feel good about myself. I had near constant stomach pain. I was eight.

Anxiety, particularly social anxiety, can be an invisible condition. Sufferers get very adept at appearing to be confident and perfectly "normal."

But the anxiety I was experiencing took on new levels, particularly when it came to contact with other people. I grew up, left home, and became a college radio DJ. Misfits like me were welcome there. If you had heard my popular radio show then, you would have thought I was very relaxed behind the microphone. Then in my twenties, I was finding my passion as a counselor in a nonprofit, landing two major promotions in the first three years. Anyone observing me would have thought I was secure, confident, and a real "go getter." That was by day. By night, I did performance art in New York City nightclubs, complete with glamorous costumes. With no acting experience, I landed a role in an independent film and later an episode of a makeover television show. It was the early days of reality TV, and the star of the movie and I were treated to gorgeous gowns and hairstyles. What I didn't realize at the time is that episode would air about a hundred times over the next two years. I learned, "Wow, people really do like makeover shows!" as I was recognized in public almost weekly. I began writing and performing spoken word poetry, competing in competitions called slams. Anyone observing me would have thought I was leading a dynamic, confident life.

But here's what wasn't so visible:

- Each week before my radio show, I would break out in a cold sweat. My hands would tremble as I pulled the records out of the library.

- I could only grocery shop at a store that was open twenty-four hours. I'd arrive about 2:00 A.M., hoping it would be deserted. If I began to walk down an aisle and found a single person there, I would leave and only return once it was empty.

- I lost many potential friendships and opportunities because I was frozen when it came to returning phone calls. I blamed myself for laziness and procrastination, when it was actually pure fear.

- When I got the role in the film, I had to call the CEO of the nonprofit I was working for. To accept the role, I would need to take a month off with only a few days' notice. I had only worked there for a year. I desperately wanted her to say no, that I could not take the time off! This way I would not have to face my fears. I could decline the opportunity of a lifetime and the director and my friends would understand. I'd have the perfect excuse. Instead, she said, "Whatever is good for you is good for the company. Have a great time." The last thing I wanted was her enlightened attitude, thank you very much! Instead of being happy, I began to shake with fear. I took the role and arrived in Toronto with a very high fever. The stress had made me very sick.

- I suffered many interminable sleepless nights when my mind just couldn't shut off, with worries playing on a perpetual loop.

- For several days before each art performance, my stomach would clench up and I'd begin dreading it. I was white-knuckling it through every routine.

- If I was alone and got recognized in public from that make-over show, I'd feel terrified and want to hide, no matter how kind the approach.

- Even though I dearly loved it, I gave up performing spoken word poetry. My voice would tighten once I got in front of the mic and I would freeze. I always left feeling embarrassed and disappointed in myself. The stage fright had gotten so intense, I just couldn't face it anymore.

When the fears surfaced, I tried to pump myself up: "I can do this! I got this!" And when that failed, I would try to talk myself down off the ledge: "I'm okay! Everything's okay!" Then I would try logic. After all, many of these fears didn't make sense: "This is a nice audience. Look, my friends are here. It's just a regular person with a shopping cart, buying food, just like I am." And when that didn't work, I'd fall into brutal self-criticism: "There's something seriously wrong with me. I screw everything up. I'm a loser. I'm a coward. I'll never achieve what I want."

I was given well-meaning advice: "Just keep pushing through. You'll develop a thick skin." (It doesn't work this way.) "Stick to your day job. You can do that." (Gee, thanks for the vote of confidence.) "Imagine the audience in their underwear." (This is just absurd.)

My nervous system was reacting like my very life was in danger. My energy default was set on anxiety. I just didn't know that at the time. Here I had been having these incredible experiences. A movie role! A glamorous makeover! Recognized in public! But I was only able to partially enjoy them because all the anxiety surrounding these situations was so intensely overwhelming. Meeting new people and having to make conversation left me tongue-tied and feeling foolish. I'd end up blurting out something ridiculous, then obsess about what I should have said for days following. My friends laughed about my "foot-in-mouth disease." I'd wake up in the middle of the night with a sense of dread, wondering how I could possibly get through that show or that meeting. For all the excitement and thrills, the fear before and after (and, at times, during) was just crippling. Feeling my heart thump so hard it made my ears vibrate was not fun.

Then, in my early thirties, I began studying EFT, Emotional Freedom Techniques. As the name suggests, this offered freedom out of my overwhelming emotions. I learned how to tap for myself and found I could calm the intensity of my feelings. Now there was something I could *do* to neutralize those fears, insecurities, and self-doubts. I started to perceive life differently, as a safe place for me. I got in touch with my own energy and found a language to describe what I had been sensing for my entire life. I just hadn't known what it was. I immersed myself into learning everything I could about how to manage my own energy, release the blocks that had been holding me back, and start living from a place of power instead of fear. I found there was a healing revolution happening!

Many years later, my life looks radically different.

■ I am a celebrated speaker in both the United States and Europe. I stand onstage, in front of hundreds of people, to spread a message of hope and healing. I often share personal stories about my own path in order to help others and do so with complete vulnerability. I don't just speak. I truly *enjoy* the entire process, from writing to orating. It satisfies me in ways other public pursuits hadn't.

- I transitioned out of a day job and steady paycheck into working full time for myself. Serving clients, writing, teaching workshops, and researching—this isn't just my job. It's my great love, my passionate vocation, and what I was always meant to do. I am fulfilled in a way I hadn't known was possible. I feel inspiration daily. Energy work allowed me to clear the fears of not having a stable income.

- I sleep well 95 percent of the time. I fall asleep easily and stay asleep soundly, waking refreshed. This, from a former lifelong insomniac.

- When my energy is balanced and I'm taking good care of myself, most of the attention deficit disorder symptomology I experienced (like an inability to focus or sit still) is gone.

- I'm able to be radically authentic. No more need to wear various masks or play roles to appease others; I experience the value of getting to be my true, unique self. I tell the truth and live with integrity according to what I believe. I say what is hard to say. Without being worried I will spontaneously combust!

- I know myself very well. I know my weak spots. I know my defense mechanisms. And I know what to do about them. I also experience my talents and gifts in ways that continue to surprise and delight me.

- I'm able to love myself and others with such depth. I've also been loved and supported by others in ways that bring tears to my eyes. Not for who they want me to be, but for who I really am. I'm able to forgive and let go of resentments and old baggage.

- People can still try to bully me. That's a common experience when you step into your power. It's sad to say this but not everyone is thrilled for you when you shine. But I healthfully and effectively stand up for myself. I never let the nonsense get in my way. I keep moving forward whether I'm being cheered or jeered.

- It's been a long, long time since that makeover TV show, so I no longer get recognized on the street. But I feel like a superstar in my own life.

- I can return phone calls, meet new people, and make new friends wherever I go. As I travel quite a bit, this has been essential.

- Then there's all the physical stuff. Chronic allergies reduced. Blood sugar beautifully balanced. Hand-eye coordination and physical balance greatly improved. A partially dislocated shoulder healed without drugs or surgery. Plus, I normally have bountiful physical energy. (And I don't normally consume caffeine or use other stimulants.)

Okay, so enough about me. Let's get back to you. What can energy healing do for *you*?

- Reduce the emotional and physical effects of stress, often dramatically and sometimes in cases when nothing else will. Stress-related conditions can then improve.

- Break limiting, defeating patterns in your life.

- Release fear in all its forms: anxiety, shock, panic, phobias, nervousness.

- Retrain your nervous system for calm.

- Demonstrate how to work with life rather than against it.

- Express and release emotions in healthy ways.

- Heal faster from illnesses, surgeries, or injuries.

- Improve physical balance.

- Lower high blood pressure.

- Focus better.

- Sleep better.

- Love more, including loving yourself.

- Be happier, period.

THIS IS EMPOWERMENT, FROM THE INSIDE OUT

Life isn't very fun when you believe you are at the mercy of the people and circumstances around you. In fact, it can feel like a huge burden. Sure, it's great when your partner arrives home from work thrilled with a new promotion. But what if they just got laid off? Or had an argument with the boss? That doesn't feel very good at all.

When we place the responsibility for how we feel on the people in our lives or how the stock market did that day or what world events we saw on the news, we can be in for a very unsettling ride. Every day can feel like a minefield. We tiptoe through this field trying not to set something or someone off, hoping peace will be on the other side. But there is no other side. You may have already realized this approach doesn't work very well. We will never be able to exert enough control over the people and world around us so we can feel good. It just doesn't work that way.

When you focus on balancing your own energy and releasing old blocks, you begin living from the inside out rather than from the outside in. Taking responsibility for your own feelings—because, after all, they are indeed yours—and finding ways to make yourself feel better is very empowering.

You can make changes in your energy field and this changes how you feel. No special equipment necessary.

What new choices would you make if you knew no matter what the outcome, you'd be okay? Win or lose, triumph or perish, you knew you'd be just fine? That you could release fear, worry, shame, anger, and embarrassment? That you could embrace change? That you could let go of old resentments and truly forgive? What would you do?

Would you create a business?

Start dating again?

Mend that friendship?

How about write that book?

Here I am, writing this book for you all. And every day I am using the practices I will be teaching you here so I can actually get the job done. I've been a writer since I was a child and yet this is my first book, oh so many years later. My first book contract. With a prestigious publisher. And a very short deadline. Yikes! I can assure you, there was a time many years ago when the fear and self-doubt would have caused me to sabotage this precious opportunity. This incredible chance to share with the world what I love and trust more than anything would have been lost. Or, to be truly honest, I likely wouldn't have been able to say yes, to even try it. But here I am, saying yes, and making it happen. And I have energy healing to thank for it.

I balance my energy every morning. When I am balanced, creative ideas flow more easily. I tap on fears and self-doubts. Paying attention to that inner critical voice while tapping gets it out of my way. It clears the thoughts long enough for me to remember how confident and capable I actually am.

I tap on procrastination. You know you're procrastinating when you would rather do your taxes than write your book! Facing that impulse, tapping on the resistance to my dream, allows me to make progress. If my mind wanders and I lose focus, I get my energy crossing over again so I can get back to it. When I finish writing, I ground myself. That way I can be present for the other tasks in my life, from working with a client to making dinner to paying bills.

Yes, dream-making, fear-shaking, illness-breaking changes *can* happen for you. Healing is a process, and most positive changes on long-term conditions will take some time. But you can begin feeling lighter and more relaxed today, right away, in a matter of minutes.

You bring your body with you wherever you go, carrying powerful tools and wisdom. You experience energy all day, every day. Is there any better time than now to learn how to work with it?

PART II

* * * *

ENERGY HEALING PRACTICES

{ 5 }

GENERAL PRINCIPLES ABOUT WORKING WITH ENERGY

Here are general principles to keep in my mind as you embark on the wonderful world of energy healing.

1 + 1 = WAY MORE THAN 2

Clients are often surprised that the homework processes I assign don't feel as impactful as when we do them together. In session, they are more easily able to feel the shifts and sensations that are happening in their energy fields. Then, on their own, the processes feel a bit flat. But there's a good reason for that. Whenever two or more people come together, whether that's in a spiritual practice like prayer or energy practices like the ones in this book, the effects are amplified. That amplification is more than double when it's two people and grows exponentially the more people are participating. This is why energy-moving practices like tai chi and qigong are most often done in large groups, especially in the East. In fact, in China it's not uncommon to find crowds of one hundred or more outside, doing tai chi in unison. Imagine the Electric Slide of relaxation and balance.

Energy Healing with a Friend

If you have a curious and open-minded friend or partner in your life, invite them to do some of these practices along with you. It will be easier to feel the benefits as they are happening. And if you're able to experience those shifts and how good they feel, you'll be more likely to make them part of your everyday life. Plus, partners and friends that tap, cross over, and balance together stay together. You will be in sync with each other and this makes for an easier, happier relationship.

Energy Healing with Children

These practices are great to do with kids! If you can catch them young enough, before age nine or so, they will usually do them without much fuss and often with great enthusiasm. That's because they don't yet have much self-consciousness. And children, like us, enjoy anything that makes them feel good. If you have teenagers, they will likely not want to practice with you. Don't take it personally! But I wish more than anything that I had EFT and these other practices when I was a teen. My entire adolescence would have been dramatically better. So, don't be shy about introducing them to this book. They may end up reminding *you* that it's a good time to tap.

Energy Healing on Your Own: What This Book Is About

Having shared the above, please know that all of these practices are designed to do on your own. No friend or child necessary. I'm spelling that out so you're not tempted to use it as an excuse: "Oh, I live alone. Can't try any of these!" Our minds are adept at looking for reasons to not try anything new. Learning something new can feel awkward and clumsy, like learning a new language. You *are* learning a new language: the language of your energy.

When you're working as a solitary practitioner, remember that consistency is key. The more you do these practices, the better you will feel. Try one daily for a couple weeks. Then don't do it. It's often when you *stop* doing the practice that you realize how much it was doing for you.

The Snowball Rolling Downhill

Just like a snowball that gets bigger and rolls faster the farther it goes downhill, energy work can feel the same. The more balanced you get, the easier it is to reach that state, and the deeper the benefits feel. The more blockages you release, the more you're able to release, and the deeper the releasing will be. This is good to know when you're getting started. The shifts may feel subtle in the beginning, but know you are building momentum.

6

BASICS FOR A SAFE AND EFFECTIVE PRACTICE

GROUNDING

Grounding integrates the different levels of your energy system. The easiest way to know what grounding is is to experience what it feels like when you're not grounded.

Symptoms of Being Ungrounded

Trouble focusing

Feeling spaced out or getting "the stares" (staring off into space)

Clumsiness (for me this was constantly walking through doors and hitting my shoulder on the side of the doorway)

Poor balance

Being so stuck in your thoughts you don't remember what you just did, like your drive home (Allow me to emphasize here: this is not good!)

Feeling over wired and over tired

Feeling unsafe

Feeling disconnected

Why We Get Ungrounded

Too much time indoors

EMFs (electromagnetic frequencies)

Stress/trauma

Feeling unsafe or insecure

Overthinking; living in our heads and not our bodies

Consuming stimulants like caffeine and sugar or anything your body doesn't tolerate well (gluten is a common one for many)

Benefits of a Regular Grounding Practice

Calming

Reduces inflammation in the body

Helps increase focus

Can help with releasing excess weight (a body can put on weight to ground itself)

Enhances sleep

Enhances energetic and physical balance in the body

How to Ground

- Walk with your bare feet on the ground. If the dirt or grass is a little damp, that will create even faster grounding. Feel the earth supporting you.

- Walk outside consciously. Focus on each step as it makes contact with the ground.

- Rub and tap on the bottoms of your feet. Stamp them up and down. Jump up and down, focusing on the sensation of your feet making contact with the ground.

- Use magnets or metal on your feet, especially the bottoms of the feet. Anything with a magnetic charge will ground your energy. Rub or place them on your feet.

YOU CAN USE:

Refrigerator magnets

Professional magnets like Nikken

Hematite crystals (shiny and metallic charcoal in color)

A metal spoon

- Do a **Grounding Meditation**. Imagine there's one cord attached to your tailbone and two on the bottoms of your feet. Imagine bringing these cords down through the floor beneath you, into the earth, through layers of rock, sand, dirt, and water, until it reaches the earth's fiery center. Place a large anchor there and attach your cords to it.

- Take a warm bath with 1 cup of sea salt and 1 cup of baking soda. Besides grounding, it detoxes your body as well. If you don't want to soak your whole body or don't have a bathtub, use a plastic basin to soak your feet and ankles. Cut the portions of sea salt and baking soda down to about a ¼ cup each.

- Slap or pat the outside of your body. Become conscious of the outside of your body and use your hands to pat, rub, and/or lightly slap yourself. Start at the upper body and move down to the feet.

- Give yourself a hug and feel the squeeze.

FEELING ENERGY

Any energy practices you do will benefit from your ability to feel what is happening, even if it's subtle. It's easier than you imagine. As you're made of energy, it's within and all around you, all the time. In the beginning, it can feel like the proverbial fish searching for water, unaware that it's everywhere. The following are steps that can guide your efforts to experience your own energy and the energy around you.

Intention

Set an intention to be able to have a deeper and more conscious experience of your energy. Here are a few intentions you can use:

1. My intention is to be able to feel energetic changes and shifts in my body.

2. My intention is to be able to receive and understand energetic information about myself, others, and the environments I am in.

3. My intention is to focus on creating greater energetic flow in my body and feeling all the benefits that gives me.

These can be seen as a framework. You can change the wording to best reflect how you speak. Place one hand on top of the other in the center of the chest and speak one or more out loud.

Don't underestimate the power of setting intentions. This is one of those practices that is so simple, you think, "What could this *possibly* do?" It would be good for you to face that inner naysayer now anyway. It will pop up throughout our time together, not just with intention setting. You will read a process and before you can even try it, there that voice will be, telling you, "This won't work. It's too simple." I'm going to encourage you to welcome the voice of your naysayer. Hear it out. Allow it. *Then try everything anyway.*

Getting Conscious

Being conscious to what is happening within and around us isn't easy! There are constant lures to plug in, tune out, and live in our heads. These distractions can be quite seductive and addictive. Intellectual information and logic can serve in many ways. But as I saw on a meme once, some questions can't be answered by Google! That includes the search engine in our left brains. In fact, energetic information may be contrary to what your logic is saying.

Here's an example of how being tuned in to your energy is helpful in an everyday situation. After a meal in a restaurant, you check the receipt. Everything appears to be in order and your logical mind considers the matter closed. But energetically, something feels off or just not right. Now, there's no evidence to support that. It's just a mild feeling in your stomach area that you can't define. You make a note of it. Later you check your credit card statement online and see you've been double charged. *Your energy does not lie.* It is interacting with the energy in all people and experiences. It gives you very important information that can save you time, money, and even a whole lot of heartache. Listening to it will benefit every area of your life.

Ways to Get Conscious

1. **Focus on Your Breath.** Close your eyes. Bring all awareness to your breath. Follow the cool air as it enters your nostrils, then travels down to expand the lungs. Feel as the lungs then contract and the air travels back up to be released through the nose. This exercise will cause your mind to wander. When you notice that has happened, simply return to following the breath without any self-criticism. Try this for two minutes, once a day, for a couple of weeks.

2. **Truths and Lies.** Beliefs about honesty can vary by culture. One of my best friends is from Holland. The quality I like best in her is her ability to just say the truth and do so in a direct manner. No sugar coating, which is a very Dutch quality. When she is living in the United States, she has found this isn't always appreciated. In the United States, we tend to say things we don't necessarily mean, under the guise of being nice. Like suggesting an undefined lunch date to an acquaintance, when there's no intention of making that happen. It seems quite innocent and just becomes an unconscious habit. We tell ourselves we are being kind, even noble; that it's the way to get along well with others. The truth is, on an energetic level, that person knows you're not being sincere. Honesty and falsehoods have great consequences on our energy fields. Telling the truth allows our energy to expand. Lying causes it to contract.

   Start with an intention to be more aware when you're telling the truth and when you're lying. Please suspend all judgment of yourself about this. Lying causes your energy to contract. If you then beat up on yourself about it, self-criticism will make it contract even further. This is an energy exercise, not a moral inventory. How do you feel when you've told the truth? How do you feel after you've lied? See if you're able to feel that expansion or contraction.

It will be easier to choose telling the truth when you know what the consequences are. You can find kinder ways to do it. It may not be easy in the beginning, but the freedom it brings feels awesome!

Now that you've been getting more conscious, these simple exercises will help you feel energy.

Hand-Rubbing Exercise

1. Place your hands palm to palm, as if in a prayer position.

2. Rub them vigorously, back and forth, against each other for about a minute or so.

3. Back in the prayer position, focus on the palms. Feel the heat, tingling, or any other sensations that may be present.

4. Slowly move the palms apart, about an inch.

5. Then slowly bring the palms back together again.

6. Now slowly move them farther apart, about 5 to 6 inches.

7. Then slowly bring back together again.

8. Pay attention to the palms and what they are feeling.

9. As you pull the hands apart, feel the energy between them, stretching like saltwater taffy.

10. As you bring them back together again, feel how the energy is squeezed until overflowing past the hands.

11. Continue this exercise, slowly and consciously bringing the hands out farther and farther apart, then back together again.

12. Now bring the palms about a foot away from your face. Close your eyes and slowly begin to bring the hands toward you until they are about 6 inches away.

13. Experience what your hands are feeling as you move them closer. Experience what your face is feeling as the hands get closer.

14. Move the hands to about 6 inches from the top of the head. Move slightly closer, then slightly farther away.

15. Move the hands to the back of the head about 2 inches from the scalp. Bring the hands up and down, feeling the energy present.

16. Bring the hands to the front of the chest and begin moving closer to the heart area. Feel your hands and your heart area.

17. Place your hands palms down on the thighs and rub them. Stamp your feet a little to get grounded.

18. If you don't feel anything the first time you try it, this exercise can be repeated once a day. You will soon be able to feel what's happening in that invisible space between the hands.

Step-by-Step Exercise

This is a simple walking exercise that helps you recognize your own energy as it makes contact with the energy of the ground.

1. Go for a walk outside. If you can get out into nature with limited distractions, do it. If you're a city dweller, try this with noise-canceling headphones.

2. As you step down, focus on the bottom of your feet making contact with the ground.

3. Feel each step as it lands and then rebounds back as the next step touches the ground. Make each step slow enough that you can remain conscious while stepping.

4. Do this for about ten minutes, a few times a week.

Sensing the Senses

These are all about getting out of your head and into your body during everyday tasks.

1. Shower: When you're taking a shower or bath, feel the water against your skin. What does it feel like running through your hair, against your shoulders, falling onto your feet?

2. Eating: See the food before you. Take in the colors, the shapes. After you place it into your mouth, close your eyes. I know this is a radical idea, but truly *taste* your food! Feel the temperature, the textures, the flavors. Chew longer than you normally would and swallow consciously.

3. Chores: Pick a chore you normally do mindlessly, like doing the dishes or folding clothes. Feel the water on your hands, the weight of the dish, or the texture of the fabric.

You're doing them anyway. Might as well make them a part of your journey. Don't underestimate the power of these. You may be amazed what just a few minutes of focus can do for you.

THE ENERGY OF EMOTION: FEEL THE FEELINGS

If this heading were written on a whiteboard, I'd be circling it in huge loops and putting stars all around it. The value of this practice is immeasurable. This is an exercise that I give my clients because it teaches them that they are not at the mercy of their emotions. I could say that a thousand times. But me saying it and them experiencing it on their own are quite different. Feelings allowed to flow are healthy, even when they are uncomfortable. I made this a part of my regular energy practices years ago and it allows me to live with so much freedom. If you take nothing else from the book, try this one. It is very powerful.

Have you ever seen a baby get angry? This adorable little person transforms before your eyes, getting red-faced, scrunching up their brow, balling up their fists, screeching at you from the top of their lungs like you owe them money! Then within minutes, the eruption has passed. The inner storm ends. Their face smooths out and color returns to normal. And they might even start laughing, a full, bubbly belly laugh. That's how quickly you could process your emotions as well. The difference between adults and babies is most babies allow emotions to flow. Especially if they haven't been told not to cry by their well-meaning caregivers. They let out the emotion in all its fullness, without resistance. A baby does not care if you are in line at Whole Foods. A baby will express without shame. This usually starts to change when children enter the toddler stage. Suddenly their emotional reactions have noticeable consequences. They are aware of the discomfort of their parents. They start judging themselves for having these disruptive, unacceptable emotions.

I'd love to see a world where the children in our lives are able to experience their full spectrum of emotions. When emotions are allowed to flow freely, the energy of them doesn't get stuck in the body. I know parents can feel great pain witnessing the upset in their little ones. If this is true for you, allow *your* feelings about *their* feelings. First allow them. Then in addition, you can tap on them. (See Chapter 8, page 95 on Emotional Freedom Techniques.) And yes, absolutely be a soothing comfort for them. But allow their feelings to flow without judging or halting the process. They will learn that it's safe to feel anything and everything and still be okay. They can grow up to be happier adults as a result.

The energy of our feelings gets stuck because it's human nature to avoid pain. Those patterns start early. A painful experience occurs and before there's even a moment for a conscious choice, that person is off to the bar for happy hour. It happens automatically. This is the behavior behind all addictions. People avoid the discomfort of their feelings in so many ways. Overworking, overeating, overthinking. But what we resist persists.

This practice allows the energy of all emotions to simply *be*. When they are allowed, they move. When they move, they release and transform.

Feeling Your Feelings Exercise

1. **Choose the right time to start.** The right time is when you are experiencing uncomfortable emotion from a recent situation. Supervisor called you out in a meeting? Car broke down? Huge, unexpected bill arrived in the mail? GREAT. It's just what you need to get started. Don't worry. You won't be feeling enraged, sad, or anxious for long.

2. **Get comfortable.** Drink water, grab some tissues, and get seated in a comfortable position.

3. **Check in.** Scan your body and see how you feel.

4. **Bring up the painful situation and relive it in your mind,** starting at just before this bad thing happened. For the bill example, you would start at sorting the mail.

5. **Allow.** Allow the story. Allow the thoughts and evidence your mind has been gathering. Allow whatever feelings there are to become fully present.

6. **Drop out of the story in your mind and down into the sensations of your body.** This is where you are feeling the effects of that story/memory.

7. **Feel the sensations.** Three main areas to check on are the throat, chest, and stomach areas, although the energy of that emotion could be anywhere from your head to big toe. What does it feel like? Heaviness, tightness, like you got socked in the stomach? Is the energy tingly, chaotic, hard, cold, or stringy? If the answer to that question is anxiety, then I'd ask, what does anxiety feel like in your body? How do you know you're feeling anxious? Let go of the labels and just feel.

8. **Move into the sensations.** Bring all of your awareness to these sensations. Just be with them. Don't try to make them be any different than they are. Allow them as is. If the feelings are quite strong, you may only be able to do this for thirty seconds. Good. Then do it for those thirty seconds. Do it for as long as you are able. If tears come up, cry. Tears are our natural, built-in release system at work. They are there to do their jobs. Don't forget to breathe, in through the nose and out through the mouth.

9. **Follow the energy.** The sensations may move. If they do, follow them. Just bring your awareness to wherever the energy leads you. Again, do not try to shift, release, or change anything. Just be with it. And breathe.

10. **Give it space.** Imagine you are giving this energy space in all directions, space it may need to flow.

11. **Experience the energy flowing.** If you're able to stay with the sen-

sations, you will experience the energy of the emotions shift on its own. Where there was heaviness, it's now light. Where it was hard, it's now soft.

12. **Return to the story.** Get back into your head and relive what happened. Does it feel the same? Are you having those same painful thoughts about it? If any pain remains, repeat the process. You may want to check into the story each day, allowing the energy to be there, then witness its moves until it finally feels released.

See how you can combine this with tapping in Chapter 8, page 95.

STUCK?

If you find yourself complaining about the same scenario over and over again, try this exercise. As long as you're in the story in your head, you're not in the feelings about it. Maybe there's a coworker who constantly takes credit for your work. If your friends' eyes are starting to glaze over as you recount the latest incident, it's time for a different approach. Being stuck in a situation means you have stuck energy. Feeling the feelings allows movement internally so that changes can then happen externally. Close your eyes and begin that same story, saying it out loud. Do this long enough until you begin to feel the pain about it. Then close your eyes, drop the story, scan your body, and note what's happening.

LEFT/RIGHT REPATTERNING

One of the most valuable principles I've learned from energy pioneer Donna Eden is that our energy is designed to cross over from side to side. The left and right sides of our energy field can get stuck, with the right side running on the right side and the left running on the left. I've come to find this is epidemic. When in this state, 50 percent of your physical energy is not available to you and that includes the energy you need to heal or create the life you desire. Once you get your energy crossing over consistently, many persistent, chronic conditions of all kinds, from depression to allergies, become easier to shift.

In all my years of practice, I have only found one client whose energy was consistently crossing over. He's a brilliant conductor and musician. My best assumption is that when he conducts or plays, his energy has to cross over to be able to perform the required functions. Musicians *are* making two different movements with their hands, and moving a baton back and forth creates a crossing-over effect. From years of practice and performances, his energy likely got trained to mostly stay that way.

Then there's the rest of us. My energy was running in a homolateral pattern for most of my life. This meant I was clumsy and accident-prone. I couldn't jump rope with the other kids, as I felt off kilter each time my feet landed on the ground. And my timing was way off, as I'd land *on* the rope, much to the dismay of my playground cohorts. I would walk into the corners of walls. I developed a pattern of reversing letters and numbers, much like those with dyslexia. This lasted until a few years ago, when I got myself crossed over and made a practice of tuning it up each morning. When I'm writing and notice I've started reversing letters again, it's a red flag, but easy enough to correct. I do one of the following exercises:

Cross-Over Exercises

1. Swing Walking
   a. Walk while swinging your arms vigorously. As you take a step with the left foot, swing your right arm, then

reverse, just like marching. Bring the arms up over the midline of the body.

b. Do this for a minimum of ten minutes.

QUICK TIP: **When blocked while writing or brainstorming, do this to get your creative juices flowing again.**

When I work with creatives, I encourage them to do this whenever they get stuck while working on a project. I had learned over the years how this short, vigorous walk always broke up my writer's block. I'd return to the page with solutions and fresh eyes. I just didn't know why it worked. Getting the energy crossed over and both hemispheres of the brain working well together allows creativity to flow once again.

2. The Infinity Press Down

Imagine a squared-off infinity symbol. Press and drag your hand in this pattern:

a. Place your dominant hand on your left hip. Press it in with some pressure.

b. Drag it across to the right hip and up to the right side of the torso.

c. Then drag it straight across the center of the torso, just above the belly button, to the left side of the torso.

d. Drag it up the left side of the body to the upper chest, just past the armpit, then straight across to the right armpit area.

e. Then drag that hand down to the middle of the right side of the torso and drag across the center line again.

f. Finish by dragging the hand down to the left hip where you started.

g. Repeat 4–10 times.

The Crossing Over Brain

Having your energy crossing over helps the left and right hemispheres of your brain work well together. The left and right hemispheres of the brain perform different functions.

THE LEFT-BRAIN QUALITIES

Analysis

Logic

Reasoning

Interprets language and numbers

Used in math and science

THE RIGHT-BRAIN QUALITIES

Creativity

Imagination

Intuition

Used for art and music

To enhance the hemispheres' connectivity, try the following exercises.

1. If you are right-handed, start doing more activities with your left hand to stimulate the right brain. If you are left-handed, start doing more activities with your right hand to stimulate the left brain. Each hand influences the side of the brain that is opposite to it.

   Back when I used a mouse for my computer, I trained myself to use it with my left hand so that this would enhance my right brain. I had been working on a series of clay sculptures and wanted to enhance my creativity. My art that year was the best I had ever created.

Even tasks as simple as using your non-dominant hand to open and close cabinets, press buttons on the remote, or pull laundry out of the washer or dryer can make a difference. It will feel awkward at first, but you'll also be more conscious while you are doing it, an added bonus.

2. Visualize. Visualizations can actually move energy. Have fun creating greater connectivity by visualizing one of the following: Visualize roads that are placed horizontally across the two hemispheres. See tiny cars traveling back and forth with trailers on the back carrying information. See bundles of tiny letters and numbers going from the left side to the right side. See tiny music notes, paintings, and colors traveling from the right to the left, like they are sharing their gifts with one another. See electric wires connecting both sides of the brain. Imagine light moving through the wires from one side to the other.

CLEARING AND SHIELDING

Every day we come into contact with energy that can greatly influence our mood and well-being. Have you ever walked into a party that was bubbly with fun and excitement? You immediately felt at ease and got swept up in the revelry. Or have you ever found yourself at an unfortunate Mary Tyler Moore party? I call them that affectionately. On the TV show of the same name, Mary always threw these terrible parties. Her friends dragged themselves in and got into arguments with one another. No one had a good time. The energy of such an event feels dead, heavy, and forced.

Many years before I knew anything about energy, I spent the day in a hospital with a friend who was awaiting surgery. Each hour, the surgery was further delayed and, as she was unable to eat or drink, I didn't eat or drink anything either. Finally, at the end of the day, they wheeled her down to the operating room. I was instructed by the nurses to check in on a lower-floor waiting room before I went to get a bite to eat. This way they could contact me if I was needed. The waiting room was quite large with a round nurses' station in the center. As I entered the room, all of the color drained from my face and I felt my legs begin to buckle beneath me. The feelings of anxiety and pain in that room were completely overwhelming! I spun around immediately, grasped the doorway, and collapsed into a folding chair just outside of the room.

I knew what the problem was in an instant. For decades, beloved family members and friends had sat in that room, worried terribly about their loved ones who were in surgery. That anxiety had been building up for years. And I could feel it! I'm sure my experience was made more dramatic because I hadn't eaten all day. But I will share that this is not a unique experience. I've felt similar energy in every hospital waiting room I've been in since. The only difference between me and the other people in those rooms is that I'm more conscious of it, so I'm able to feel what's in the energy around us all. Hospitals just don't know about the energy of emotion and how it needs to be cleared. If they did, hospitals could become far healthier environments for patients and their families.

I share this story for two important reasons. I want you to know that highly toxic energy can build up in many environments, including your own home. If you or anyone in your household has been sick, stressed, or depressed, it's even *more* important to clear. I hope you'll be inspired to create a practice of clearing your own home regularly. The second reason is so you will take steps to shield yourself energetically every day and reinforce that shield when entering places like hospitals, prisons, or even concert halls and bars. Wherever people congregate, there will be collective energy in that space. Often it can contain what you'd rather not be picking up on and feeling.

Clearing Your Energy Field

Before clearing any space, clear your own energy first. Just like you regularly cleanse your body and teeth, it's important to cleanse the funky, gunky energy that's in your field. Some of it will invariably be yours, from your own stress, illness, or painful emotions. Some will be what you've picked up from other people and places. Think of it as energy hygiene. I clear myself in the morning, between clients, and at the end of each day.

Visualization

This can be done anywhere, any time, even while sitting in a busy airport, a place I do this practice often. If you think you're not good at visualizing, give it a try. Like anything, it gets easier with practice. Plus, you're not just imagining, you are creating a real energetic shift that you will be able to feel in time.

If you are religious or spiritual, you can ask for divine help for this process.

1. Set an intention for releasing all your own negative energy and everything you've picked up from others. I like to say: *I am easily releasing all energy from myself and others that no longer serves me. I do this for my highest good.*

2. Imagine a small ball of brilliant, golden light in the center of your chest.

3. Imagine breathing in and out through your chest, expanding the light on each exhalation.

4. Spread the light throughout your entire body. See it in your head, torso, arms, and toes.

5. Now expand it beyond your skin until the light is about an arm's length out in all directions.

6. Follow by shielding (instructions on page 62).

It is that simple and it *does* work. When done regularly, you will find yourself calmer, less reactive, and more balanced overall.

SEA SALT/BAKING SODA BATHS

Dissolve 1 cup of sea salt and 1 cup of baking soda in a warm tub and soak your toxicity away. You can use this mixture as a foot soak instead, cutting the sea salt and baking soda down to about ¼ cup each. It's also good for your skin and very grounding. (See page 40 for more information on grounding.)

ENERGY HEALING PRACTICE FOR CLEARING

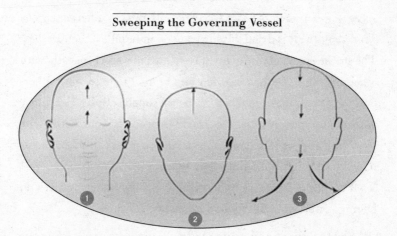

Sweeping the Governing Vessel

1. Place the middle fingertips of both hands on the forehead, in between the eyebrows.

2. Trace them up the center of the forehead, across the top of the head (imagine the line if your hair were parted in the middle), and down the middle of the back of your head, until you reach where your neck connects to your shoulders. Then sweep each hand across each shoulder. Left hand sweeps across the left side of the shoulder. The right hand sweeps across the right.

3. Breathe in through the nose and out through the mouth while doing this.

Clearing Your Space

With all of the following exercises, set a clear intention for clearing first. Going through the motions won't create satisfying results if you're not aligned with why you are doing it. Intention itself shifts energy.

SAGE

Sage is a common herb that has been used to clear the energy of spaces for thousands of years. Clearing with sage is called smudging. Traditionally, it is dried, often wrapped in bundles, then burned. The smoke is spread into every inch of area in a space, usually with a handheld fan, feather, or dried bird wing. I tend to warn others not to get hung up on purchasing special supplies. Space clearing is natural and most of what you need is already in your home. The sage itself can be purchased in spiritual stores, health food stores like Whole Foods, gardening centers, and even on Amazon.

Practice good safety by burning in a fireproof container and having water available for dowsing when finished.

1. Start by smudging yourself first. Using your hand, bring the smoke close to your body. Spread it across the body, over the

head, under the arms, and then lift a foot, one at a time, and place it in the smoke. To do your back, blow into the burning bundle and then turn around in it.

2. Now bring the smoke into every area of your home, including closets and cabinets.

3. At the end, open a window and allow the smoke to dissipate.

4. Put out the sage.

Note: The scent of sage can be quite strong and the people around you may think you're smoking marijuana. The scents are similar. There are also spaces where it is not appropriate to burn anything, like an office building, for example. (To avoid a potentially embarrassing situation, look for those sprinklers overhead.)

If you or anyone in your household has a lung condition, know there are other ways to smudge, without smoke. I rarely burn sage anymore. I got tired of people asking, "Have you just left a bonfire?" I use a spray that contains essential oil of sage and sea salt. It works perfectly.

SALT WATER

Get a spray bottle and fill with distilled water and sea salt. Shake until the salt is dissolved and use as you would the sage. Understand that your space may get damp. You can add a few drops of cleansing essential oils like lavender, eucalyptus, or sage.

PRAYER OR SPIRITUAL PRACTICES

Work within your own religious and/or spiritual beliefs here. Pray and invite the higher being or beings of your tradition to purify and cleanse you and your home of all energy that does not serve you.

If you come from a spiritual background that uses incense, that can be used as part of your cleansing. Use as you would use sage.

Shielding

I am a giant sponge. Wherever I go, I soak up whatever is around me. When it comes to learning, this is an asset, as I absorb information from classes and books quite quickly and deeply. When it comes to the rest of my life, it's a definite liability! When I did volunteer work in a prison, I would leave in a state of great sorrow and even, at times, physical pain. I concluded I was just too sensitive to remain volunteering there. I didn't know how to shield myself then. Now there's nowhere I can't safely go.

Some of us are more spongy and porous than others. But *everyone* picks up energy.

If you're a compassionate and sensitive person, you may believe taking on another's stuff is beneficial and a positive thing to do. The person whose gunk you're taking on may temporarily feel better, but ultimately you *cannot* do their healing for them. This is energetic codependency. You may derive good feelings from helping others, while at the same time it's harming you. I've had a number of healer, social worker, activist clients for whom this was true and I've seen the results firsthand. It's not good. It can lead to chronic illness and depression or, at the very least, loss of a zest for life. If this resonates, I recommend attending a free twelve-step program called Co-Dependents Anonymous (see Resources section in the back of the book). This is a pattern that is likely not just happening energetically, and you can free yourself. Becoming compromised makes you of little use to yourself *and* others. It's important all helper-giver types learn to give from their fullness and not when depleted. Taking on others' energy *will* deplete you.

When I encounter people who already know about shielding, I can find a common mistake in their practice. They forget to shield until they are in a situation where they feel themselves taking on another's stuff. Say you're sharing a meal with a friend. That friend is going through a breakup and clearly angry and depressed. Suddenly you start to feel tired and edgy when before dinner you had felt upbeat. *Now* you remember to shield! You can do one of these processes, but by now you've zipped up their gunk into your energy field.

Remember:

- Cleanse first

- *Then* shield

With the example above, I'd recommend excusing yourself, going to the restroom, clearing, shielding, then returning.

SHIELDING VISUALIZATION

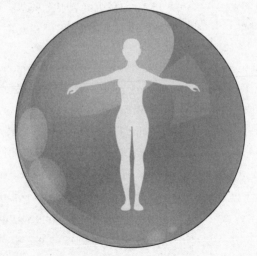

1. Imagine a large bubble around you, about an arm's length from your body in all directions.

2. See this bubble as a solid wall or a filter that covers you completely. Ask this bubble (or shield) to act as a cell wall, using its intelligence to allow love and positive energy in. Ask that

anything negative not be allowed in, to hit the shield, slide off, and get neutralized by the earth. (Another option is to imagine mirrors on the outside of the shield, so anything sent your way gets reflected back to the person who sent it. Frankly, I'd like less negative energy in the world and prefer my method above.)

3. Fill the bubble with golden light.

MUSCLE TESTING

Your subconscious mind is a brilliant database. Imagine a part of you that records every single experience you've ever had, including what is out of eyesight. Right now, as you're reading and your conscious mind is focused on this content, your subconscious registers the crack in the ceiling paint, a pet approaching from behind, and the sound of a car alarm going off in the distance.

I got to see just what the subconscious is capable of several years ago. I was napping on my couch while the television was on. One of those afternoon talk shows was playing. As I slept, I had this very vivid dream about Harry Connick Jr., the famous singer. He was sitting in an old college classroom of mine, speaking with my favorite professor. He talked about his new album and the city of New Orleans's influence on his style of music. My professor was nodding along and asking the obvious questions, like the album's release date. Just then, outside my apartment, a loud siren ran past and I was awakened with a start. There was Harry, on my screen, being interviewed about his new album. He looked exactly the way he did in my dream and the information about his album's title and style was accurate. My subconscious mind had recorded it all and changed the setting to a classroom and replaced the talk show host with my professor. This was a valuable lesson for me. Even though my eyes were closed, and my conscious mind was asleep, I was taking in everything on that screen, including commercials. No wonder I suddenly had a craving for soda, just like what was advertised on TV! This is a beverage I've never liked and don't drink.

This is not something I do now. When I watch television and movies, I do so consciously, and I use a DVR so I can screen out the commercials. My subconscious mind is a potent, creative force and has more important things to do than encourage me to buy more stuff. Commercials are actually designed to influence your subconscious mind, even more than your conscious one, to encourage purchase of their products.

I actively use my subconscious mind for:

- Uncovering old wounds, limiting beliefs and unhealthy programs so they can be neutralized. I think of it as deleting a file from my hard drive.

- Manifesting the feelings and experiences I desire. I create new programs to run based on feeling good about myself and life.

Finding that "old gunk" I want to delete is much easier since I learned how to muscle test.

EXPANSION AND CONTRACTION

When you are around people you love and situations that feel good, your energy expands. It opens and grows, becoming more inviting, like a flower in full bloom. When encountering anything or anyone that feels bad or unsafe, your energy contracts. It closes off. Shrinks. Withers. Your energy field is perpetually in a state of expansion and contraction, responding to the stimuli it meets. That stimuli includes everything from your living environment and the people you see, to music you listen to, foods you eat, anything you read or watch on a screen, and stores you visit. Throughout the day, your energy field is indicating what feels good and what feels bad by expanding and contracting, just like you avoid people who drag you down and run toward those that make you smile. Your actions toward others are an indication of what is happening on a deep level within you. If you are able to recognize when this is happening, you can read your body's responses to get valuable information.

Muscle testing is a way of reading the body's answers to different stimuli.

There are dozens of different muscle-testing methods. If you have a friend to practice with, start with the Arm Test.

THE ARM TEST: FOR YOU AND A FRIEND

As you are the person reading this book, you will start as the test*er* and your friend will be the test*ee*.

1. Have your friend stand up straight with feet hip-width apart. Have him or her raise one arm at a ninety-degree angle from the shoulder. Rather than placing it straight in front, or directly to the side, split the difference and place it in-between. Only muscle test an arm that is injury- and pain-free. Be sure to ask your friend if he or she has any arm or shoulder problems before proceeding.

2. Place one hand gently on the shoulder you're not using. Place the index, middle, and ring finger of your free hand on the wrist that is raised.

3. Ask him or her to say "My name is [their name]" out loud while you gently press on the wrist. Their arm should stay up or test strong.*

4. Then ask him or her to say, "My name is Sassafras." (Unless their name *is* Sassafras, of course, then have them say any name that is *not* theirs.) You're testing the lie here. Their arm should go down or test weak.

5. Now do a silent test. Have your friend think of someone they don't like. It can be a politician or their boss. But ask them to just think about the person rather than say anything out loud. Muscle test in the same way. They should test weak.

6. Now do the opposite. Have them think of someone they really love. Pets or children are wonderful examples for this exercise. Muscle test in the same way. They should test strong.

7. Now reverse roles and do all of the steps. When having your friend test you, close your eyes and feel what's happening in the rest of your body as you test weak and strong.

*If your friend tests weak when they say their name and strong when they lie, their energy needs rebalancing. (See What if my *Yes* is a *No* and my *No* is a *Yes*? on page 72.)

I love to do this one with very strong men. It's great fun to show a body builder that I can lower his massive bicep with two little fingers, simply by having him tell a lie! It's clear I'm not as physically strong as him, so it's very eye-opening.

The Sway Test: For Yourself

The easiest way to begin muscle testing by yourself is with the Sway Test. Don't do this if you have vertigo or a problem with basic balance.

Before the test, choose two substances to test: one you know is beneficial for you and one you know is probably not. Foods are good for this one. Most organic produce will test strong unless you have an intolerance to it. Most products with chemicals will test weak. I'd hate to be responsible for a breakup between you and your Pop-Tarts, but know that can happen with this test. When you feel how your system goes weak with certain foods, you may rethink what you're eating. (Actually, I wouldn't hate that at all. I'm pulling for you and your happily balanced energy!) To really feel a weak test, use bug spray or any toxic chemical.

1. Stand up straight with your feet together. If it's difficult to bring your feet close enough that the sides are touching, bring them as close together as possible where you are still comfortable.

2. Close your eyes and do a brief check-in to see how you feel.

3. Say a statement you know is true, like "My name is [your name]" or "I am [your age] years old."

4. Feel if you begin to sway slightly forward at speaking this true statement. Note how you feel inside when you say it, not just the motion of your body moving forward.

5. Now say a statement you know is not true, like "My name is Marilyn Monroe" or "I am three years old."

6. Feel if you begin to sway slightly backward at speaking this false statement. Note how you feel inside when you say it, not just the motion of your body moving backward.

7. If you sway forward when speaking the truth and backward when you're not, your energy is likely running in the right direction. Proceed with the next steps. If not, see page 72.

8. Now test the substances. Start with the positive one.

9. Reinforce the subconscious response to the positive substance. Bring the positive substance up and down several dozen times. As you bring it up, say out loud "This is a yes" while swaying

forward. Place the substance back at your side. Bring it back up and say again "This is a yes" while swaying forward again. You can do this quickly. A hundred times should take less than two minutes.

10. Reinforce the subconscious response to the negative substance. Bring the negative substance up and down several dozen times. As you bring it up, say out loud "This is a no" while swaying backward. Place the substance back at your side. Bring it back up and say again "This is a no" while swaying backward again. You can do this quickly. A hundred times should take less than two minutes.

You are training the subconscious mind to let you know what is a yes and what is a no, just like the substances you are testing. The sways should be gentle but noticeable. Do this once or twice a day for a week or two. It will reinforce your body's response.

Muscle testing is not 100 percent accurate. If you strongly believe that something is true, even when it is not, you can throw the results. If you're under a lot of stress, tired, or dehydrated, this can also influence the answers you get. A way of bypassing your own will and ideas to get to the truth is to conduct a blind muscle test.

Blind Muscle Testing for Answers

1. Think of a question you'd like help answering.
   A couple examples:
   The reason(s) you haven't been sleeping well the past week
   What foods your body likes and doesn't like
   The best place to go on vacation

2. Cut several equal-sized pieces from sheets of paper.

3. Create a list of every possible answer you can think of that could be true or all possibilities you are considering.

4. Include an option that you already know is 100 percent false. If it tests as a *no*, then you know the other answers are likely correct. If it tests as a *yes*, then you need to balance your energy before retesting.

5. Write one item on each piece of paper.

6. Include a piece that says "Other." If the answer is something you had not thought of, this allows the subconscious to indicate that.

7. Fold each piece in the same way. Place in a bowl.

8. Pull out one folded piece at a time without looking at it, hold it to your chest and test. Place all the *yes*es in one pile and all the *no*s in another. You may get one or two that test in the middle—not a complete no, not a complete yes. Put any like this in its own pile.

9. When done, read the results.

What does a "middle" answer indicate? The answer is partially true or is unclear to the subconscious. You can ask follow-up questions about it.

BLIND MUSCLE TESTING FOR SUBSTANCES

One of the most amazing qualities about the human energy system is how specific it is to each person. Your energy field knows what is compatible with your body and what is not. There will be foods, environments, and supplements that are supposed to be healthy for you, but if these items are not in resonance with your energy, they could actually make you unwell. And the opposite could be true for someone else.

There seems to be so much confusion these days about how to be healthy. We are so fortunate to live during a time when boundless information on diet, exercise, and nutrients is available. It seems almost everyone I know is taking some kind of supplement, like turmeric for joint inflammation or vitamin D for the immune system. Muscle testing these supplements can save you money, time, and maybe even a stomachache or other bad physical reaction.

1. Get a sample from each of the items you want to test.

2. Place one sample in its own white envelope.

3. I like to include an item I know will test weak. For me, that's a packet of artificial sweetener. If it tests weak, then I know the other answers are likely correct. If it tests strong, then I need to rebalance my energy before retesting.

4. Place the strong and weak results in separate piles.

5. Open the envelopes to see the results.

What if you test weak on a supplement you need or would like to take?

1. Consider another brand that sells the same item and muscle test it.

2. Find another type of supplement that is known for similar effects. For example, if turmeric tests weak, try cinnamon for reducing inflammation instead. You can even create an entire list of supplements that are believed to do that. Then muscle test to see which one your body prefers.

3. Unless prescribed by a licensed health professional, listen to your body and just stop taking it.
   OR

4. Come into energetic alignment with it. This can be very effective. (See page 76)

WHAT IF MY *YES* IS A *NO* AND MY *NO* IS A *YES?*— POLARITY BALANCERS

Energy can get reversed and move in the wrong direction. This is called polarity reversal. It's easier for this to happen than you can imagine. If you are tired, dehydrated, or sensitive to EMFs, that can be enough to throw your energy off. (EMFs are electromagnetic fields that are experienced in increasing volume due to the wide use of Wi-Fi and electronics.) And of course, our old nemesis stress can have a huge effect as well. Thankfully, it is quite simple to correct. Do any of the following.

1. The Thymus Thump

    Using a fist, thump on your breastbone or sternum, located in the center of the upper part of the chest. Do one firm thump, followed by two softer thumps, then repeat. Think of a waltz: ONE, two, three, ONE, two, three. Repeat about five or six times, breathing in through the nose and out through the mouth.

2. Polarity Balancer #1

    ▪ Place one hand against the abdomen with the palm directly against the belly button.

    ▪ With your other hand, place the thumb on one collarbone point and the fingers on the other collarbone point. (To see and learn about where this is, see the EFT points on page 103 and description on page 104.) Rub vigorously for about a minute while breathing in through the nose and out through the mouth.

    ▪ Repeat the same actions by switching hands.

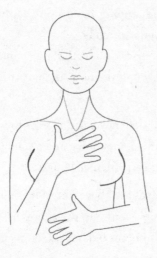

3. Polarity Balancer #2
   - Place one hand against the abdomen with the palm directly against the belly button.
   - Take the index finger of the other hand and place under the nose and above the upper lip (see page 103). Take the middle finger and place on the crease of the chin. Rub these two areas for about a minute while breathing in through the nose and out through the mouth.
   - Repeat the same actions by switching hands.

4. Polarity Balancer #3
   - On one hand, bring all the fingertips together, like you're trying to pick up a small bead.
   - Place those scrunched-together fingertips one inch below the belly button.
   - Use the fingers on your free hand to tap the fleshy side of the hand on the belly. You'll be under the pinky finger. Tap for about twenty seconds.

- Bring the tapping hand up to tap under the nose for about twenty seconds.
- Alternate back and forth for a couple minutes, breathing in through the nose and out through the mouth.

5. Drink water!

Getting hydrated may be all it takes to reverse course. Adding fresh, organic lemon juice and a pinch of sea salt to your drinking water can enhance hydration.

After doing one of the above, retest using the muscle-testing methods to make sure your energy is moving in the right direction. If it's not, try another balancer. Get good quality sleep and then try again the following day.

Polarity balancers aren't just for correction when muscle testing has gone awry. Having your energy running in the proper direction is fundamental to any other energy work you do, or really work of any kind. Familiarize yourself with them and make one a start to your practice. They only take a couple minutes and will ensure your success.

> QUICK TIP: During your morning shower, do a polarity balancer. You'll be sure to start the day with your energy moving in the right direction.

Muscle Testing Uses

Everyday Uses

- Deciding which entrée to order in a restaurant*
- Choosing a vacation destination
- Choosing which workshops to take, books to read, or movies to watch
- Finding the best route on a map

- Finding specific events in your past that relate to a current condition

- Discovering limiting beliefs

- Evaluating what percentage a condition has been healed

- Discovering the next best step in your healing journey

- Knowing the right lifestyle changes needed to heal (diet, exercise, energy practices, health professionals to see, stress management techniques, etc.)

*I was out to dinner with two energy medicine friends. I couldn't decide what I wanted to order, so I muscle tested three choices. One was a clear *no*. I just assumed my body wouldn't tolerate it well. One of my friends ordered that same dish and when it arrived, it was clearly spoiled!

Muscle Testing Misuses

- **Future Events** Life is constantly changing. You can muscle test to predict a possible outcome, but between now and then circumstances may change that would affect the answer.

  Example: If I muscle test for how much magnesium I should take daily for the next two weeks, the answer will be based on how much magnesium I need at that moment. If, the following day, I eat several magnesium-rich foods, I will likely not need to take that amount. I may not need any additional magnesium at all.

  You can use muscle testing to give you an idea, but know that can change at any time. Muscle testing is not fortune-telling.

- **Questions About Other People** Muscle testing measures your resonance with a question, idea, substance, or environment. It's not for finding out information about other people, unless you are using yourself as a surrogate to test another's resonance. (I don't recommend this for beginners.) When you realize that your body gives accurate answers, the normal temptation is to ask it *everything*. "Eureka! I'm a walking lie detector!" This can include questions like "Did he leave me because I'm boring?" or "Is she married?" Your attachment to the outcome isn't going to give you accurate information anyway. These questions are not appropriate. Respect others' privacy just as you like yours being respected.

Energetic Alignment with Food and Substances

Whatever I put in my mouth, whether that's food, supplements, or even a medication, it's important that my body accept it. I want the food I eat to nourish my cells and give me energy. I want supplements or any medication I may be taking to perform their functions perfectly, making me feel better. But there are times when our energy systems are not in alignment with these substances. It can happen for physical reasons, like if there's a chemical in the food the body doesn't like. Or it can happen for emotional reasons as well. Say you were eating an orange when you got a phone call with shocking news. Your nervous system could make an association between the orange and the shock, causing inflammation or itching whenever you now eat one. That harmless orange has been identified and labeled as a serious threat. But there are energetic ways to break those associations and get innocent substances off the "no consume" list.

1. Get a sample of the food or supplement and place it somewhere on your body so it's making contact. True confession: I usually stick it in the center of my bra. But you can place it

on your lap or under your sleeve. If the substance needs to be in a container, like with a liquid or powder, use glass instead of plastic.

2. **VISUAL LEARNERS:** Imagine a picture of yourself on the left side of your vision and an enlarged image of the substance on the right side of your vision. Tap the EFT points for three rounds while looking at this mental image (page 103).

    KINESTHETIC LEARNERS: Scan your body and energy field prior to making contact with the substance. Then place it on your body. Pay attention to any changes you may feel, like nausea in the stomach or tension in your shoulders. Focus on the discomfort and tap the EFT points until there's a shift.

3. **BOTH VISUAL AND KINESTHETIC LEARNERS:** Tap three rounds on the EFT points while saying out loud, "This [orange, etc.] is safe." (See diagram on page 103.)

4. Retest. If you now test strong, congratulations! Your body and energy field are in alignment with that substance. If it tests weak, repeat the exercise and test again. If it remains weak, listen to your body and just stop taking it or eating it for now. This applies to foods and supplements only, not medications. Always take medications as prescribed by a licensed health professional. You may want to ask your doctor if there's another medication you can take in place of the current one. I've seen clients who were not resonating with a generic version of a drug resonate nicely with the name-brand version of it.

7

CALMING THE NERVOUS SYSTEM

S tress is a red-hot topic right now. It seems people are more stressed than ever before. We *are* living in a time of great change, where familiar ways of being are shifting dramatically. What used to feel certain now feels highly unknown. Family, cultural, political, economic, and religious structures that were in place for hundreds of years are breaking apart, evolving, and transforming before our eyes. It's an exciting time to be alive when we have choices available to us that have never been known before. Then there's the chaos that comes with great change. From natural disasters to acts of violence, people are on edge.

The known effects of stress on health are numerous, contributing to headaches, digestive problems, diabetes, obesity, heart disease, and even neurological conditions like Alzheimer's disease. Leaving stress unchecked comes at a mighty high price.

Psychologists have also known for decades that even very positive changes cause great stress. From marrying to moving to getting that new dream job, it can take time to find the new normal.

But what is stress?

You know it as tension or worries. You experience it as overwhelming. You see it as the result of problems or having too much to do. But you may not know what's happening in your body. When we look at stress, it's important to understand the physical and emotional consequences.

There are two parts to the nervous system.

- Somatic nervous system is the part of the nervous system that voluntarily responds to external stimuli.

- Autonomic nervous system is the part of the nervous system that involuntarily regulates internal body functions.

The autonomic nervous system (think *automatic*) is divided into two parts:

1. Sympathetic
2. Parasympathetic

THE SYMPATHETIC NERVOUS SYSTEM (FIGHT OR FLIGHT)

The focus of the sympathetic nervous system is survival. If you were crossing the street with a baby in your arms and suddenly see a car barreling toward you going a hundred miles per hour, this system would automatically and instantaneously perform complex physical responses to ensure your safety. In an instant, you'd be given everything needed to leap out of the way, saving your life and the life of the baby.

What it does:

- Controls the fight, flight, or freeze response

- Prepares the body for intense physical activity like fighting or fleeing an attacker. Blood rushes to the arms and legs. Heart rate increases.

- Causes the liver to release glucose for quick energy

- Dilates the lungs to increase oxygen

- Dilates the pupils of the eyes to take in more information

- Secretes epinephrine (commonly known as adrenaline) and norepinephrine* from the adrenal glands, hormones that help with all the above activities

- Stops digestion, even if you've just eaten a full meal

*Both epinephrine and norepinephrine are neurotransmitters that act as hormones. They have powerful effects on the body, increasing blood sugar levels, heart rates, and the squeezing of the heart. Norepinephrine alone increases blood pressure. Having too much and too little of these powerhouses can cause or exacerbate major health problems.

THE PARASYMPATHETIC NERVOUS SYSTEM (REST AND DIGEST)

This is the state we'd like our nervous system to be in most of the time. Imagine walking into a crowded shopping center to meet a new friend. You calmly scan the crowds, feeling completely safe and at ease. A mother with a toddler accidently bumps into you and you smile, stepping to the side to make room for her. You find your friend and learn that the restaurant you'd planned on eating at has an hour-long wait for a table. No matter! You and your friend decide to explore a few stores. The conversation flows easily, and you feel comfortable being yourself. When you finally sit down for dinner, you're able to eat slowly, savoring your food. That night you gently fall asleep.

What it does:

- Relaxes the body and allows rest

- Decreases heart rate

- Stops releasing glucose from the liver

- Contracts the lungs as extra oxygen is not needed

- Contracts the pupils of the eyes

- Stops secreting epinephrine (commonly known as adrenaline) and norepinephrine from the adrenal glands

- Helps you feel safe.

- Allows digestion. Nutrients can be fully utilized.

Thankfully, in modern times, most people are not living in constant and immediate danger. Yet this brilliant defense mechanism is still within us, ready to act at any time. It becomes problematic when it is overactive, reacting to situations that are not life threatening.

I had an intense experience of this recently. First, there's something you need to know about me. I am a full-out, true-blue book junkie. Hard-core. The fact that I am finally writing a book makes more sense than a lot of other choices in my life! I have a library in my home and I follow authors I love like they're superstars. You wanna rock my world? Send me a signed book! Words are my friends and I like to have a lot of those friends around me.

A few weeks ago, I attended an event for an author I truly admire. Months before, I had signed up to hear her speak and get my books signed. That morning I got ready like I was going on a date, applying an extra coat of mascara, dancing in my kitchen as I pulsed my smoothie. I was bringing several of her books for signing. The event space was lovely, with lots of natural light and calming colors. The author's presentation was funny, inspiring, and joyful, as she read aloud and answered questions from people in the audience. My energy was very open because I was feeling warm, loving, and safe. About two thirds of the way into her talk, she gave thanks to the people in the room who were there to support her, like her husband and friends. Then she announced that a person was there whom I had never expected to be present. Let's just say they were someone I used to know. Before my mind was even able to fully digest this information, my nervous system went into a full-blown fight-or-flight response. At the same time, there was a part of me that became the witness to the experience and found it fascinating! "Wow, look at what my body is doing!" While the rest of me wanted to leap up and run screaming out of there! My mind went completely blank. It made sense, as blood was rushing from my head and torso into my arms and legs. My heart began to pound so loudly I could hear it vibrating in my ears. The muscles in my chest began to contract. And I felt like I had gotten socked hard in the stomach. My entire energy field contracted, along with my muscles, as I witnessed my shoulders inching up toward my ears and my back rounding down toward my lap, going into a protective posture. I remembered there was a camera behind me that was live streaming the event to thousands of others. My fear of public humiliation was only slightly higher than the terror of staying put. Plus, I was squeezed into a sold-out room. It wouldn't be easy fleeing. Thankfully, due to my training and experience, I knew exactly what was happening and precisely what to do about it. Sitting right there, in my seat, invisible to anyone else, I was able to calm down that reaction enough that I was able to stay. My heart rate returned to normal. My body began to uncoil. The fear lessened by about 75 percent. All of this in fifteen minutes. I wouldn't say the rest of the event was sheer joy for me. A complex chemical reaction had been set loose in my body and I was still feeling some of its effects. But I was no longer reacting as if my very survival was in danger, like a gun had been pointed to my head. I remained until the end and did get my precious books signed.

I'm sure you're wondering why this even happened. There had been a time years before when that person had been unkind to me. It certainly wasn't anything remotely life threatening or physical in any way. I had just felt humiliated and disrespected at the time. Because I had felt awful afterward, I did energy work around the specific circumstances to neutralize it. I wanted my healthy self-esteem back. And everything felt complete at the time. Whenever this person came up in my email or was mentioned by a mutual friend, I actually felt at peace with them and what had happened. There are times when people further our healing in ways that are painful, and this was one of those times. I got that. Although not fun, it was an essential part of my growth and my life had moved forward in the most incredible ways since. This person furthered my evolution and I was truly, sincerely grateful for that. Yet that all changed instantaneously when we surprisingly ended up in the same room together, after all this time. My reaction was not logical. Not at all. Emotions never are. I was not in danger in any way. But my energy field and body were responding as if I was. It was just very important that I manage and heal that reaction, calm my nervous system, and come back into balance. And I was able to do just that.

After the event, I ran several blocks back to my car to burn off some of that excess adrenaline. I sat in my car and tapped until I came back to a place of peace. Then I had a good cry, releasing all the remaining pent-up energy. I had a good night's sleep and by the next day, I was back to my happy self.

There was a time in my life when I would have run screaming out of the room. Or tried to stifle the symptoms until it felt like a full-blown panic attack. And there's *no way* I would have been able to stay for that book signing. I would have missed out! And felt lousy for hours, days, or even weeks afterward. My practice is filled with people who are still suffering from the effects of painful reactions they experienced long ago. I'm here to tell you, it doesn't have to be this way.

There are simple practices you can do to move back into parasympathetic mode anytime it's needed.

The Shhhh Technique

As an Energy Coach, it serves me well to have lots of energy-healing friends who are as passionate about this stuff as I am. We just love to "talk shop," exploring ideas, experimenting, and sharing tips. This technique is a favorite that I've learned in one of those sharing sessions.

It is easy to remember, highly effective, and works fast. It's also effortlessly done in front of others without alerting anyone to what you're doing.

I call it the Shhhh Technique. Because something isn't anything until you give it a name. Plus, I'll happily no longer have anyone ask me to "show that finger thing." The action you take is similar to when you're shushing someone. It also describes its purpose in quieting the nervous system, moving from a sympathetic to parasympathetic response. Think of it as shushing your jumpy and edgy feelings.

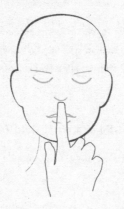

1. Whenever you're feeling nervous or anxious, do a quick scan to see how that nervousness is presenting in the body. Are your palms sweaty? Is your leg bouncing up and down? Take note.

2. Bring your index finger up to your face.

3. Line it up with the fingertip starting just under the nose. The rest of the finger will go over the lips and chin, in a straight line.

4. Press that finger in and breathe in and out through the nose for a couple of minutes.

5. Pay attention to what that relaxation response feels like. Normally you can feel a shift within just a few breaths.

6. If you're doing this in public, rest your thumb on one side of the chin and curl the other fingers and rest on the opposite

side of the chin. For added effect, you can slightly furrow your brow. This makes you look like you're concentrating or thinking deeply. No one will know you're calming yourself.

7. Afterward, do another scan and note how you now feel.

> QUICK TIP: Do this prior to eating. As the sympathetic nervous system shuts off digestion and the parasympathetic allows digestion, doing this before a meal will make for far more productive absorption and elimination.

The Fingertip and Wrist Hold Technique

This process is gentle and easy, and yet it's a powerful stress reliever.

1. Start by taking the four fingers of your dominant hand and wrapping them snugly around the thumb of your non-dominant hand. Be sure to make contact with the last segment of the finger that contains the nail. Your grip should be firm but not painful.

2. Breathe in through the nose and out through the mouth. Wait until you feel a shift or experience a yawn. (Not everyone will experience this. For some, a shift may be subtler. Thirty seconds is usually more than enough time for a shift.)

3. Repeat for the index finger.

4. Repeat for the middle finger.

5. Repeat for the ring finger.

6. Repeat for the pinky finger.

7. Now repeat the process. Start with wrapping the fingers of your non-dominant hand snugly around the upper part of the thumb of your dominant hand.

8. Breathe in through the nose and out through the mouth. Wait until you feel a shift or experience a yawn. (Not everyone will experience this. For some, a shift may be subtler. Thirty seconds is usually more than enough time.)

9. Repeat for the index finger.

10. Repeat for the middle finger.

11. Repeat for the ring finger.

12. Repeat for the pinky finger.

13. Now wrap your dominant hand around the inside of the non-dominant wrist and hold.

14. Breathe in through the nose and out through the mouth. Wait until you feel a shift or experience a yawn.

15. Repeat with the non-dominant hand wrapped around the inside of the dominant wrist and hold.

16. Breathe in through the nose and out through the mouth. Wait until you feel a shift or experience a yawn.

> **PRIVACY TIP:** This can be done in front of others without anyone knowing what you're doing. As you're holding the thumb, allow the fingers of that hand to gently rest on the hand that's doing the holding. Hold your hands in your lap. I like to do this one on the subway and no one has noticed yet. (That *may* not be the best test, though. You have to do something dramatic to get attention on a New York City subway!)

Chilling Out the Triple Heater Meridian

There's a powerful meridian in Traditional Chinese Medicine called Triple Heater, also known as Triple Warmer or Triple Burner. The three "burner" areas are the thorax, abdomen, and pelvis. It's responsible for heating and cooling the body and governs respiration, digestion, and elimination. This meridian is unique in that it can control all of other meridians. It also has a major impact on the immune system.

Imagine Triple Heater as your energetic defense system. When Triple Heater is balanced and functioning properly, it lies somewhat dormant, calmly doing its job. When it senses a threat, Triple Heater goes on the defensive, temporarily taking energy from the spleen meridian to get supercharged and defend its territory. Then it chills and waits for the next potential threat. Except when it isn't able to do that. Triple Heater can easily become overactive and overprotective. This produces problems. For one, it causes the spleen meridian to be constantly depleted. Our spleen is fundamental to both our immune functioning and digestion. That's on a physical level. On an emotional level, a strong spleen meridian gives us courage. A depleted spleen meridian makes us feel anxious and hopeless, and contributes to low self-esteem. It can make it very difficult to change. Triple Heater bases what is safe on your current circumstances and wants them to remain the same. But we live in a time of constant change and Triple Heater is confronted with relentless stimulation, world events, chemicals, toxins, and other strangers it wasn't designed to face. It's no wonder Triple Heater can be on the continual defensive.

I see so many clients in my practice who are seeking to make major changes in their lives. They can't seem to understand why they aren't able to get out of their own way. But the real blockage is happening on an energetic level. Triple Heater senses change as a threat, gets reactive, and depletes spleen. Now they feel wired, anxious, and sick to their stomach every time they try to take steps forward. And spleen is the meridian of courage. All changes require great courage. My clients feel like failures, when the truth is they're trying to drive across the country with an empty gas tank. I have them cool Triple Heater daily, encouraging a new pattern of calmness. Then they can start to make changes. If Triple Heater gets reactive again, they will now be able to feel the effects, where previously those feelings were just normal. They can return to these practices again and again to energetically signal Triple Heater, and the rest of the body, that these changes are not a threat.

Triple Heater meridians start at the ring finger, go across the back of the hand, along the side of the forearm, along the back of the upper arm, across the shoulder, up the side of the neck, around the ear, and end at the temple.

1. Massaging the Gamut Point

    (See EFT diagram on page 103.) Take the index finger of your dominant hand and place it in the space between the pinky and ring finger of your non-dominant hand. Drag the index finger down onto the back of the hand, passing between the knuckles. You will feel a hollow space in between the bones that connect to the ring and pinky fingers. I like to think of it as a tunnel or ditch.

    Rather than tapping, I encourage you to use stronger pressure for this. Rub vigorously back and forth or deeply press into this area.

    Breathe in through the nose and out through the mouth.

> **PRIVACY TIP:** This can easily be done in public. Hold the point in and breathe. It will look like you are simply holding your own hand.

2. Massaging Around the Ears

Breathing in through the nose and out through the mouth, start at the temple and massage the scalp in the area surrounding the ears. I like to take two fingers and massage in small circles, starting at the temple and traveling around the ear until I reach the area behind my earlobe.

3. Tracing Triple Heater Backward

Do one side at a time.

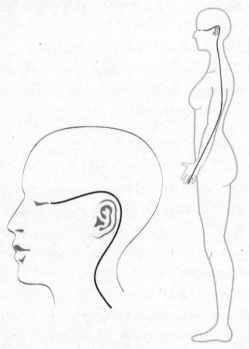

- Bring the fingers of your right hand up to the left temple. Breathe in through the nose and out through the mouth.
- Next, breathe in through the nose, and as you exhale through the mouth, trace the pathway of the meridian

around the ear, down the side of the neck, across the shoulder, down the back of the upper arm, down the side of the forearm, across the back of the hand, down the ring finger. Pinch off at the end of the ring finger and shake out the right hand. Repeat 3–9 times. See if you yawn or feel a shift.

- Repeat on the opposite side. Bring the fingers of the left hand up to the right temple. Always start with one inhalation through the nose and exhalation through the mouth first.
- Next, breathe in through the nose, and as you exhale through the mouth, trace the pathway of the meridian around the ear, down the side of the neck, across the shoulder, down the back of the upper arm, down the side of the forearm, across the back of the hand, down the ring finger. Pinch off at the end of the ring finger and shake out the left hand. Repeat 3–9 times. See if you yawn or feel a shift.
- Finish with two deep breaths in through the nose and out through the mouth.

Enhance Triple Heater cooling by speaking calming, reassuring messages to yourself while you're doing any of the exercises. I know, it sounds ridiculous, but you've come this far with me, right? Like everything else I recommend in this book, I always encourage you to try it and then see for yourself what the results are. And honestly, aren't you already speaking to yourself throughout the day? How many of those messages are loving, encouraging, and kind? Might be a refreshing change to feed yourself supportive messages.

Examples:

"I am safe. My body is safe."

"Everything is okay."

"I am protected."

"I'm aware of what's happening and I am taking great care of myself."

"It's safe to relax. It's safe to let go."

"Thank you, Triple Heater, for protecting me. It's safe for you to relax now."

Ideal Times to Chill Out Triple Heater

You're experiencing stress

You want to change a bad habit

Before eating (aids digestion)

After a workout or any physical exertion (moving furniture, lifting heavy boxes, etc.)

After a shock (bad news, an accident, a fall)

While you're watching anything on your TV or computer. Listen, you're just sitting there. You might as well make that time useful. Definitely do one of these if you're watching anything frightening or stressful (horror movies, the news, a political debate, anything with tragic or violent content, fictional or real).

Before bed (aids restful sleep)

If you have regular bouts of anxiety, a weight problem, insomnia, an autoimmune condition, allergies, or digestive disorders, consider making Triple Heater coolers a part of your daily life.

With regular practice, you will find:

What normally causes you stress just doesn't affect you the same way anymore

Taking positive actions are easier; bad habits released, healthy habits created

Experience deeper feelings of well-being

Less defensive and unnecessarily self-protective in relationships

Less overreactive to circumstances. Situations come into proper perspective. In other words, you stop sweating the small stuff. And you don't numb out or avoid when major circumstances occur that require your full attention.

Digestion and sleep improve

My client Tomas came to see me with a financial challenge. He worked in sales and wasn't earning enough to make his position secure. He thought energy work could release unconscious blocks he may have had to making more money. Within the first session, I realized Tomas didn't have a money problem, he had a Triple Heater problem. The dips in his career and finances were simply side effects of near constant fight-or-flight responses he was experiencing. His sales quotas changed daily. Every time he looked at them, Triple Heater was immediately on the defensive. Remember, Triple Heater likes everything to remain the same. He'd see the figures and begin to panic, making his sales calls from a place of desperation. To quote the movie *Singles*, "Desperation is the world's worst cologne." The energy of that desperation literally repels everyone who comes into close proximity to it. Experienced salespeople will tell you that they never sell well when they most need to. Each time Tomas didn't make the quota, he began to panic about losing his job. The fear energy was increasing and building on itself. This affected his sleep. He would wake up every night at 3:00 A.M. with racing, repetitive thoughts of poverty and doom, unable to escape them. His immune system suffered, and he was often sick, missing work and potential sales. The first practices I showed him were Triple Heater coolers. Before I could get to the underlying cause of his sales panic, I needed Triple Heater to back down and give us some room to work. Within three days, he was sleeping through the night. Within three sessions, we had uncovered and neutralized two major life events that had kept his energy set on lack. Within two months, he was making, and exceeding, his sales quotas.

A note on sleep: A healthy emotional and physical life requires healthy sleep. If you have a shock or panic that disrupts your sleep, the lack of sleep will increase your fearful feelings the next day. Then your next night's sleep is even worse. And so the cycle continues. Make good sleep a priority. Much of what you're learning in this book, including Triple Heater coolers, will help. Your energy field needs to get recharged on a daily basis and sleep is where that happens.

8

EFT
(EMOTIONAL FREEDOM TECHNIQUES)

HISTORY AND BACKGROUND

One of the main tools I use in my practice is called EFT, short for
Emotional Freedom Techniques, or more commonly referred to
as tapping. It is easy to learn, incredibly effective, and requires
no special equipment. EFT was born when a Stanford-trained engineer named Gary Craig took a course in TFT, or Thought
Field Therapy.

Created by psychologist Dr. Roger Callahan, Thought Field
Therapy used acupressure tapping on certain meridians to alleviate everything from headaches to phobias. Dr. Callahan had had
a client, referred to as "Mary," with a severe water phobia. Mary

struggled with simple everyday tasks like taking baths, and even felt nervous when it rained. This fear had been with her since she was a baby. He tried everything from traditional psychology to help her, including therapy sessions by his swimming pool that he believed would desensitize her. The best he could get her to do was dangle her feet in the water, which she did with great anxiety. She often described how she felt the anxiety in her stomach. Dr. Callahan had learned about the meridians used in acupuncture and knew the stomach meridian end points were under the eyes. On a hunch, he tried an experiment and asked to tap under her eyes as she described the fear. Much to his amazement and hers, she described the phobia as gone and ran toward his swimming pool. Concerned she would drown, he stopped her, and she said she knew she couldn't swim. She stepped into the pool up to her knees and knew for sure her fear was gone. This was over thirty years ago and she remains fear-free.

Dr. Callahan knew he was on to something important! He began experimenting with other clients and found meridian tapping effective for not just phobias but for alleviating the pain of traumas and even physical conditions. He created a series of algorithms, or tapping recipes, where you tap on specific points in a specific order. Each condition has its own algorithm.

Gary Craig learned TFT and was astounded with the results. He also saw new possibilities. What if, instead of following a specific algorithm for various conditions, you used just one tapping sequence that stimulated most of the major meridians? He thought for sure you would encounter the energetic block that was causing the problem and be able to alleviate it.

Based on one of TFT's trauma algorithms, he created EFT, Emotional Freedom Techniques. EFT was designed to be so simple, it could be learned in a few minutes. He traveled around the country teaching and doing demonstrations. EFT was proving to be incredibly effective in alleviating stress and pain.

Focus on a problem. Focus on the feelings that problem brings up. Break the problem down into small, specific pieces. Measure the intensity. Tap. Measure the intensity again. Keep tapping and testing the intensity until the feelings are resolved.

You could be crying, experiencing real sorrow, only to be laughing fifteen minutes later. This could occur after thoroughly tapping on that problem. Physical pain decreased or disappeared, just by focusing on it and tapping. Painful memories were resolved energetically. EFT was clearly working and, at times, amazingly well.

I first experienced EFT when I was working part time for a hypnotherapist in the late '90s. I was lamenting a painful pattern in my romantic relationships. I was only in my twenties but was beginning to realize the only thing my former boyfriends had in common was me! I was learning to take responsibility for my life and to stop blaming everyone else for my problems. But how could I resolve this? My hypnotherapist boss said, "I want to do this process with you. Let's see if it helps." She didn't call it EFT. She didn't call it anything. She started by asking me how I felt about this pattern and leading me through spoken phrases about the pattern while we tapped together. I was shocked! As a hypnotherapist, she was well trained in how thinking and speaking influences the subconscious mind. She was always reminding me to be more positive. Now she was having me say all these "negative" statements. When I challenged her, she said, "I understand your concerns. I don't know how this works, but it does work." I've always been incredibly curious and willing to try anything, so I decided to fully experience it. We tapped. I got angry. We tapped some more and I got sad. At one point I burst into tears. But at the end

I felt lighter and more at ease about it all. I couldn't say anything had changed except the way I felt and viewed my previous romantic experiences. I no longer felt powerless. My perception had shifted. It was only a couple of years later, after I had been in and out of two more relationships, that I realized the pattern was no more. That's when I learned this mysterious practice was called EFT and I began studying it.

The original EFT method involved a Set-Up Statement that would be spoken while tapping the side of the hand or rubbing a space on the upper chest, called the Sore Spot. Then you would tap through a series of meridian points on the body, and finish by tapping the fingertips. There was also a nine-point gamut procedure that could be done between rounds. Eventually the Sore Spot, fingertips, and gamut procedure were mostly abandoned.

DIFFERENCE BETWEEN EFT AND TAPPING

To those new to this, the terms EFT and tapping seem identical. Within the field, EFT is most often referred to as the practice and principles outlined by Gary Craig in his Gold Standard EFT. Gary generously spread the teachings of EFT across the world, allowing anyone who purchased his videotapes, then CD-ROMs, then DVDs to make one hundred copies of each and share them for free. This enabled millions of people to see for themselves the incredible shifts EFT was capable of producing. And it taught many how to begin tapping for themselves.

Tapping can mean any practice that involves tapping on meridian points. Tapping may mirror EFT in many ways and also may look quite different. As EFT was so widely shared, the many people who began using it started developing it in different ways.

Humans are quite the innovators. There are now hundreds of processes that involve tapping on meridian points.

In this chapter, I will share how to begin using the short cut version of EFT for yourself, complete with tips for making your practice effective. Then I will share a couple of tapping practices I've created to help you make major shifts. I've taught and shared these practices for a long time and they really work!

HOW TO TAP

1. **Identify the problem.** What are you seeking to resolve? What's bugging you?

   In the beginning, pick something that is relatively mild, current, and manageable. Examples of situations or conditions could be:

   - A disagreement you had with your spouse this morning
   - Anger over the car that took your parking space yesterday
   - The sinus pressure headache you've had since pollen season arrived
   - Your worry over a test you're taking this week

   These situations are not traumatic. You're not tapping on getting fired. (Not yet, anyway.) Success means starting small. It's important to crawl before you run. These examples are current. The feelings are easy to access because you are feeling them now or have felt them recently. And they are manageable because they are specific. You're not tapping on every disagreement you've ever had with your spouse, *just* the one you had this morning.

2. **Identify the feeling and rate the intensity of it.** You may be feeling many emotions, but start with one. What's on top? Anger, sadness, embarrassment? If you're having trouble accessing it, close your eyes and relive the memory of the problem you're working on. What comes up first? It's important to not censor yourself. Allow whatever feeling presents itself.

   Then give it an intensity rating. If you've been in physical pain, you may have had a doctor ask for your SUDS levels. SUDS stands for Subjective Units of Distress Scale. If a 1 means you are barely feeling the emotion and a 10 means you just want to scream, how angry or scared are you? Don't overthink this. Tune in to the emotion or pain and see what number pops up. Or use identifiers like small, medium, and large. It's important to experience how intense the feeling is so you'll be able to know if your tapping is changing it.

3. **Create the Set-Up Statement.** A Set-Up Statement begins with the words "Even though" followed by a feeling or symptom about a specific situation, and ends with an affirmation. This is the statement that is said out loud while tapping on the side of the hand.

   Examples of the beginning and middle of a Set-Up Statement:

   "Even though I'm so angry that Bob keeps forgetting to take out the trash ..."

   "Even though I'm furious that darn Mercedes stole my spot while I was waiting for it ..."

   "Even though my head is pounding because of all the pollen ..."

   "Even though I'm so worried I'm going to fail this test ..."

   Historically the ending affirmation was "I deeply and

completely accept myself." I've always liked this one because many problems in our lives come into perspective when we are able to accept ourselves and those situations rather than fighting against them. But that acceptance can be difficult! For EFT to be most effective, the statement needs to feel true for you. Feel free to use something like:

". . . this is just the way it is right now."

". . . it's just a feeling and feelings can change."

". . . I'd like to accept myself and this feeling."

". . . I'm choosing to love myself anyway."

". . . I am honoring how I feel."

Now let's put them together so we have a complete Set-Up Statement:

"Even though I'm so angry that Bob keeps forgetting to take out the trash, this is just the way it is right now."

"Even though I'm furious that darn Mercedes stole my spot while I was waiting for it, it's just a feeling and feelings can change."

"Even though my head is pounding because of all the pollen, I'd like to accept myself and let go of this pain."

"Even though I'm so worried I'm going to fail this test, I'm choosing to love myself anyway."

In the beginning, writing down your Set-Up Statement can be helpful. Be sure to use your own language for how you describe your feelings and your world. There are many flowery, eloquent examples of EFT statements online and in books, but if that's not the way you speak, those words will not be very effective for you. If English is not your first language, then experiment with tapping using the language you spoke as a child.

INCLUDE:

1. The words "Even though"
2. The feeling
3. The reason for that feeling
4. An ending affirmation

4. **The Reminder Phrase** After you've said the Set-Up Statement three times while tapping on the side of the hand, you're ready for the Reminder Phrase, which is repeated while tapping on the body points. The purpose of the Reminder Phrase is to do just that, to remind you about the feeling you are focusing on. Reminder Phrases are usually short and include the feeling. They can be as simple as "this anger" or more detailed, like "anger at Bob." Tap in a rhythmic motion on each of the body points while repeating the Reminder Phrase.

5. **Tapping Rounds** A round is the Set-Up Statement said three times as you tap on the side of the hand followed by tapping through the body points while repeating the Reminder Phrase at each point. After you've tapped on the top of the head, you've completed one round.

   Take an intensity rating at the beginning and end of each round. If after you've completed a round your intensity rating has gone down, great! Keep going and add in the word "remaining" until you get an intensity of about a 1 or a zero. For example:

   Set-Up: "Even though I still have this remaining anger at Bob, I'm honoring how I feel."

   Reminder: "This remaining anger at Bob."

   If your intensity rating has gone up, great! Keep going and add in the word "remaining" until you get an intensity of about a 1 or a zero. See example above.

Yes, when your intensity rating goes up, you are hitting the target in your tapping, just as if it's going down. Be thorough in your neutralizing and keep going.

The Points

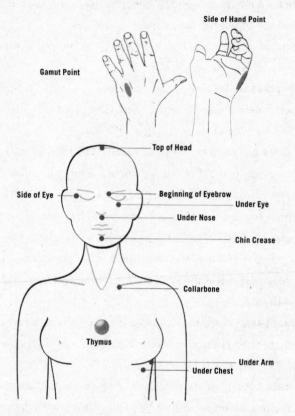

SIDE OF THE HAND: Use the fingers on your dominant hand to tap on the fleshy side of your other hand, below the pinky finger. This used to be called the Karate Chop point because that part of the hand would lead to such an action.

EYEBROW: The place where the bridge of the nose meets the beginning of each eyebrow.

SIDE OF THE EYE: Find the outer crease where the upper lid and lower lid meet, on the outside of each eye, close to the temple.

UNDER EYE: Centered under each iris, find where the soft underbelly meets the bone.

UNDER NOSE: In the center, between the bottom of the nose and the top of the upper lip.

CHIN CREASE: On the crease between the bottom lip and bulb of the chin.

COLLARBONE: Find the hard clavicle bones under where the neck meets the high upper chest. The points are just under the collarbones.

CENTER OF THE CHEST (THYMUS POINT): The hard breastbone (sternum) point that is a few inches below the collarbone points right in the center of the upper part of the chest. Ladies, think right above your cleavage. (This is a point that I have added. Tapping here stimulates the thymus gland and the immune system. As stress suppresses the immune system, I've found it to be an excellent addition.)

UNDER ARM: Place hands under your breasts, or for men, where your chest meets your abdomen, and then move those hands over to the sides of the body.

UNDER CHEST: For women, feel along where the underwire on a bra would be. It will be in alignment with your nipples along that line. For men, it's where your chest meets your abdomen in the same place. (Originally called the Under Nipple point in original EFT, it was later left out, as it was felt to be awkward in tapping. As it's associated with anger, I've found it very useful to still include.)

TOP OF HEAD: In the center of the top of the head. I often tap using a flat hand to stimulate both the right and left hemispheres of the brain in addition to the meridian point in the center.

Frequently Asked Tapping Questions

1. **How many fingers do I tap with?** The short answer is more than one. Unlike with acupuncture, where needle placement has to be exact, tapping is more forgiving. We use more than one finger to cover a larger surface area. Depending on what point I am tapping on, I use two or three fingers.

2. **How hard do I tap?** This is completely up to you. Some tap with vigorous pressure while others tap quite lightly. Don't do anything that feels painful. As long as you are seeing progress in your tapping, the amount of pressure you're using is working for you. For anyone with pain in the body, as with arthritis or fibromyalgia, know you can "tap" without actually tapping at all. Place your fingers on the point while breathing in through the nose and out through the mouth. This creates a circuit of energy.

   There are times I tap very strongly and other times when I am tender and gentle with it. Follow your intuition about what feels best.

3. **How many times do I tap on each point?** On average, 5 to 10 times per point, although you can stay on a point for far longer. If you feel a release happening, stay on that point.

4. **Do I tap with one hand or both?** This is up to you. Options available are tapping with one hand on one side of the body or using two hands and covering both sides. With the two-hand method, you can also cross your hands over as you tap. For example, using the right fingers to tap on the left collarbone point while the left fingers tap on the right collarbone point.

5. **What about tapping scripts?** Tapping scripts are written Set-Up Statements and Reminder Phrases. Created by tapping professionals, you can find thousands of them online.

Believe it or not, the subject of tapping scripts is somewhat controversial with EFT practitioners, with strong feelings on both sides.

There are many who feel that tapping scripts are just too general to be effective. Then there are others who have benefitted from them. I'm somewhere in the middle. I've used scripts for simple shifts like preventing jet lag and healing substance sensitivities. Yet when it comes to tapping for myself on emotional issues, traumas, and unhealthy patterns, using any script would be pointless. We are all unique beings with our own histories and ways of seeing the world. And my history and way of seeing the world may be even more unique than average! When I tap for myself, I am expressing my own truth. Truth is where the healing happens. I believe scripts can give interesting ideas about the multitude of approaches there are when tapping. They can provide a place to start if you feel overwhelmed or uncertain. You can always alter the language to reflect your own. Consider them research material on ways you can tap for yourself.

You will learn that it's not about the words, it's about the feelings.

What Can Happen During Tapping

1. **Yawning** This is a good sign that your tapping is clearing out energetic blockages. I tell people my business card should say, "Kris Ferraro: Professional Yawner," as I frequently yawn throughout sessions, along with my clients! It's important I let new clients know I am not tired and this is a part of the

process. If you're tapping on a particular point as a yawn comes up, stay tapping on that point until the yawn finishes. And never stifle a yawn. Others may even burp! This is physical evidence that flow is happening on an energetic level. Yawns are always good signs that you are clearing. You may also yawn with all the other practices in this book.

2. **Emotions Revealed** When we tap, we can access long-buried emotion. If tears come up, you don't have to say a thing, but do keep tapping. If tapping feels too painful, tiring, or abrupt, simply place your fingers on the points and breathe in through the nose and out through the mouth. This creates an energetic circuit that keeps the energy flowing and feels soothing at the same time. The key here is to allow the old energy of emotion to flow freely. It's ideal to tap when you have privacy and are free from interruptions so that if this happens, you can allow it without embarrassment.

3. **Energy Shifting** Certain people may feel energy flowing differently in their bodies. Perhaps you feel a tightness in the chest that feels stagnant. As you tap, it may feel like electricity is moving through the area, followed by a feeling of lightness. Look at these sensations as important information about your energy system and pay attention to shifts and changes.

4. **Changes in Perception** One of EFT's greatest gifts is called cognitive shifts. These occur when you're thinking and feeling a particular way about a person or situation and then your perception changes, often dramatically. Maybe you're worried about your daughter leaving home for college. A cognitive shift happens when the worry vanishes and you suddenly realize she is very responsible and will make wise decisions. Or you've been holding a grudge against an old friend from

college who hurt your feelings. You know it's time to let it go but just can't. Tapping on that old grievance can leave you laughing about it. Or maybe even feeling compassion for your friend. When a client says something like "Everyone makes mistakes" or "I know she was doing the best she could at the time," I know a cognitive shift has happened.

5. **Getting Tired** If you feel tired while tapping and want to stop, I encourage you to do a few more rounds first. That tiredness may be a form of inner resistance. Resistance is a part of each and every one of us. When you decide you want to feel different or make a positive change, a part of you will rise up and make itself known. It looks like procrastination or self-sabotage. That part of you wants everything to remain the same in an effort to keep you safe. For resistance, *safe* equals *same*. So now you're tapping and about to have a major breakthrough, and resistance feels like a wave of exhaustion has taken you over. If you stop tapping, you will lose momentum and that opportunity for clarity or relief may be temporarily lost. Tapping actually energizes. If you can last for a few more minutes, you may be surprised by what is on the other side of it.

6. **Getting Thirsty** When we think of energy as free flowing, images of water come to mind. Now remember that most of your body is made of this elixir and it's easy to understand how good hydration is necessary in energy work. I encourage people to drink water before, during, and for twenty-four hours after tapping sessions. Try enhancing its benefits by adding organic lemon juice and a pinch of sea salt. If you feel thirsty, then you know you haven't drunk enough.

BEFORE TAPPING: PRINCIPLES TO KEEP
IN MIND FOR AN EFFECTIVE PRACTICE
You're not upset about what you think
you're upset about . . . (not usually)

I was teaching an entry-level class on EFT when I asked for a volunteer. I needed a participant who was willing to tap with me on a current annoyance, in front of the class. I would lead the tapping, while the participant and the entire class would tap along. A man named Jake raised his hand and shared that he was completely aggravated because he'd been unable to find his watch. He was sure he put it down in the same spot he always did but could not find it before he left for work. He was clearly agitated, reporting an intensity level of 9. That's a lot of upset over a misplaced watch. I began leading him in the tapping, describing what had happened that day and how he felt about it. The anger quickly switched from the situation itself to him being very angry with himself. We tapped on those feelings and he blurted out, "I can't be trusted." Now, to me that sounded more like something a parent would say to a child, not what an adult would say about himself. As we tapped on "I can't be trusted," a memory surfaced. For his tenth birthday, he was given his grandfather's pocket watch and it had meant a great deal to him. Then he accidently overwound the watch, breaking it. His parents punished him and he wasn't allowed to have another watch for several years. The emotion of that little child had never been processed. The shame, embarrassment, disappointment, grief, and anger from decades before came to the surface and was tapped away. Two days later he emailed me and said, "I went home and there was my watch, right where I always left it." I encouraged him to consider buying himself a pocket watch.

Now that the pain was cleared, it would be a sweet way to satisfy that loss from the past. Most of Jake's upset wasn't about the current missing watch. The current experience was triggering an unhealed event from the past. EFT allows these events to be healed.

Often what is upsetting us in the present has energetic ties to unresolved pain from the past. I experience them as threads of energy that weave together experiences that have a similar emotional tone. I believe we carry around unresolved emotions because they were not able to be processed at the time they originally occurred. Something bad happened, from the mild to the horrifying. You fell out of a tree. A teacher embarrassed you in front of the class. Your little sister was hit by a car. You had to escape from a building on fire. Unprocessed emotions happen for many reasons.

We weren't taught how to allow and process our painful emotions.

Our parents didn't know how. Their parents didn't know how. Much of human history leading up to now was focused on survival. Having an emotional breakdown could make you vulnerable to violence, starvation, or abandonment by the tribe. Everyone had to keep going, keep working, keep hunting, keep providing. And if you only lived until your forties, how much baggage could you accumulate anyway?

But the world has changed. Even with the instabilities we now face, we are still living far more stable lives than those who lived even 100 or 150 years ago. My paternal grandfather immigrated to Pittsburgh from Italy. He began working in the steel mills when he was twelve. The only work I did at age twelve was babysitting and that was by choice. In just two generations in my family, everything had changed. My grandfather didn't have the luxury of time to be present to his feelings. I am so grateful that

I live in a time when I can easily free myself of the pain of the past.

Emotions are valuable information. All of them. They aren't good or bad. Some feel good and some feel bad. But they're just energy, telling us how we feel about ourselves, others, and our world.

When emotions hurt, your natural instinct is to suppress them. Your survival mechanism gets activated and says, no time for this, you have to survive. And of course, you want the discomfort to be over as quickly as possible. You may even judge yourself for having that feeling: "Only bad people get angry" or "Boys don't cry." You may be in a situation where the emotion needs to be suppressed, like in a business meeting or while caring for a child. The energy of the emotion gets blocked. It may seem like it's gone. But it's actually still being carried in your energy field.

EFT allows the energy containing that suppressed emotion to flow, processing and freeing it. Even energy around circumstances from many years ago.

Bad memory? No problem. Your conscious mind may not recall much but your subconscious holds it all. Most of my clients think they have terrible memories, only to be shocked when situations from decades before pop back into conscious awareness.

Emotions Are Not Logical

Talking yourself out of an emotional state doesn't work very well. Analyzing why you feel a certain way and how you should feel different doesn't make the feelings change. I'm sure you've tried. We all have. Emotions are not logical. They more often don't make sense than do. Trying to use logic to reason with and release that which is not logical just isn't effective.

Give yourself permission to have the feelings you have. Tapping can help change the ones that don't feel good.

Having bad feelings doesn't make you bad or weak. It just means you're having a human experience, as we all are.

Tell the Truth

Tapping works when you tell the truth about how you see and feel about a specific situation, exactly as it is. "And the truth shall set you free!" That is easier said than done. You're a good person and believe good people don't get angry. You're a strong person and believe strong people don't feel helpless. You get the idea. Be on the lookout for excuses that interfere with your truth-telling.

Enemies of Truth Excuses (hey, this would be a great band name!):

"She didn't mean it."

"He had a really hard day. He doesn't normally act this way."

"So many have been through far worse than I have."

"That happened in the past. It doesn't matter now."

"I'm such a complainer."

"It wasn't a big deal."

These truth excuses will shut down your ability to experience your feelings. These are the very feelings you're seeking to resolve.

When I speak of "the truth," I'm not referring to facts. Maybe she really *didn't* mean it and has told you so. Sure, there will *always* be others who have been through worse situations than you have. I'm talking here about *your truth*. What happened from your perspective? How do you see it? How does it make you feel *now* when you think about what happened *then*? If it's true for you, then it's true. And telling the truth while tapping allows you to access the energy blockages so flow can be reestablished.

After you've tapped, that truth—how you see and experience it now—will likely change. Don't bypass or override the truth to try and force those changes. Be present to what is and allow the shifts to be a natural side effect of the energy releasing.

How Do You Feel *Now* About What Happened *Then*?

When working on memories from the past, even if the past was just yesterday, focus on how you feel *now* about what happened *then*. Always tap on your present thoughts and feelings about past events. When you imagine what happened this morning or thirty years ago, how does it feel? Always start with where you are now. After all, now is the only time we do have.

Focus on the Feelings, Not the Words

When I began tapping, I was what I'd now refer to as a mental tapper. It made perfect sense as my background was in hypnotherapy. I was focused on changing the mental patterns in the subconscious mind. What were my negative thoughts and beliefs and how could they best be changed? As my thoughts about a circumstance changed, I felt complete. I noticed tapping calmed the emotions, but that wasn't what I was paying attention to.

Now I'm a feelings tapper. I've learned that, for me, it's not about using the right words to resolve a conflict or implant the right suggestion. The words help to access the feelings. The subconscious mind, as our inner storehouse and recorder, allows us to unearth memories and beliefs. This is valuable information in our detective work. Then I look at where the feelings about the memories are being held in the body. Once the feelings have been located and made accessible, the energy containing them can soften, open, and begin to flow. That flow is the healing you're seeking. That old bottled-up energy and the sensory information entangled in it are freed.

As you begin your tapping practice, try focusing on accessing the feelings. Use whatever words will get you there.

Be Specific, Very Specific

You're angry. You're angry about a lot of things. The economy, the environment, the job you settled for, your partner's sarcasm, the condition of your home, and the size of your thighs. That's quite a list. Tapping on "Even though I'm angry" isn't going to do much of anything. That would be called global or general tapping, and you will want to avoid this. You may temporarily feel better, for minutes or even hours afterward. Just tapping on meridian points alone, without focusing on anything at all, can uplift you. But it's not going to solve any problems.

You need to break down that anger into specific circumstances and then break down those circumstances into micro events. Let's use the example of the hated job.

- You're angry because you hate your job.

- Why do you hate your job?

    Make a list:
    — The pay is lousy.
    — Sometimes you have to work weekends.
    — Your boss is always in a bad mood.

Now break down each of these examples into specifics.

Lousy Pay

- How do you experience this?

- What about your pay makes you angry?

    — You were turned down for a raise
    — The end-of-year bonuses were canceled last December.

— Your brother told you that employees doing your job usually make $10,000 more per year than you do.

Working Weekends

- When was the last time you worked on a weekend?

- What happened that made you angry?

— You missed out on your parents' barbecue.

— It was the first beautiful day in weeks and you were stuck inside.

— Your coworker didn't show up and you had to stay longer to complete the tasks.

The Bad Mood Boss

- Think of the last time she was in a bad mood.

- What did she say or do?

— She slammed the door of her office and it startled you.

— She threw the donuts out and you had wanted one.

— She yelled at a colleague in the lunchroom, ruining your free time.

All of these anger producers have been broken down into very specific events. The most intense events in that category may not be the most recent. But it's easier to start with an event that happened recently than to think of others that are connected.

Break down large issues into specific events. Then break down those specific events into small pieces and tap on each of the pieces until neutralized.

In EFT, these individual pieces are called aspects. Clear one aspect at a time.

Test, Test, and Test Again

Tapping is effective when it's thorough. Intensity ratings are how you test how well you've cleared the energy of an event.

Take the example of the Bad Mood Boss slamming the office door. As you tap on what happened and how it made you feel, test between rounds. Bring the memory to mind. Relive it if it's not traumatic to do so. Stop tapping only after you feel relief when you think of it.

GETTING STARTED WITH TAPPING

Here are some gentle and easy ways you can begin a tapping practice.

1. **Get comfortable tapping on the points.** Increase the flow of the energy through the meridians by tapping on them and finding your rhythm. You're not focused on any emotions yet. Get comfortable knowing where they are and what your body feels like when you tap. You may want to look into a mirror when first starting.

   You can tap to the beat of the music you're listening to.
   Tap while watching a video.
   Tap while riding an exercise bike at the gym.
   Tap while going for a walk.
   Do you like tapping fast or slow? Hard or soft?

   Even though you're not focused on feelings and not actively working on a feeling, you will still get the benefit of increased energy and sense of well-being. I tap every day even when I'm not resolving anything. It keeps my energy flowing. I believe this makes clearing easier.

   Imagine a park that hasn't been cleaned in years. Trash in

the form of old newspapers, cigarette butts, and empty bottles are strewn everywhere, making it difficult to follow the path. Now imagine a park that gets cleaned weekly. Even on day six, the path will be clearer and easier to follow than if it hadn't been cleaned in months. You'll also able to walk faster on it, with less stumbling.

2. **Catch a recent upset.** You've been irked. Annoyed. Irritated. Saddened. Disappointed. It happened today or earlier in the week and it still bothers you when you think about it. Excellent! You have the perfect situation to begin tapping.

   In the beginning, taking notes can be helpful.

   - Write down exactly what happened in your own words.
   - Write down all the feelings you have about it. Or start with just one.
   - Write down all the reasons this was upsetting. There could be one or several.
   - Rate the intensity of each feeling and reason on a scale from 1–10.

   Here's an example:

   What happened: Yesterday, while walking your dog, you passed a man who was with his large dog. Unlike yours, his dog was not on a leash. His dog aggressively rushed up to yours, frightening you both. When your dog began to bark loudly in a panic, this man yelled, "You need to learn to control your animal!" You were afraid the dogs would scuffle. The other pet owner stormed off without restraining his dog. Even though no one was hurt, you're still shaken by it.

   The feelings you have (aspects): Anger, anxiety

Reasons you feel that way (aspects):

- His dog was not on a leash and this is against the law.

- He wasn't in control of his dog.

- He yelled at you for not controlling your dog when it was he who was not in control.

- You were afraid your dog would get hurt.

- You were afraid your dog would hurt his dog.

- He walked away without taking any action, leaving you to protect yourself and your dog from his dog.

- You're a woman and you felt threatened being yelled at by a man you don't know.

When you remember this event, which is stronger, the anger or the fear? Let's say the answer is fear.

When you look at the reasons, how afraid did they make you feel? Let's say "You were afraid your dog would get hurt" and "He yelled at you" were the most fearful reasons. The dog getting hurt was a 10 and being yelled at was an 8.

Start with the strongest feeling and the strongest reason. Create a thorough Set-Up Statement: "Even though yesterday I was terrified that Sweetums would be hurt by that jerk's dog, I'd like to let this go now and come back to peace."

This is a good Set-Up Statement. It's specific, contains the feeling and the reason for the feeling, and ends with a believable affirmation.

Next, tap on the body points, repeating the Reminder Phrase. The Reminder Phrase could be something like, "Terrified for Sweetums" or "Afraid he'd be hurt."

After a tapping round, retest. How strong does it feel now? Keep tapping until you get that feeling down to a 0 or 1.

If a memory surfaces, like of your childhood dog being bit by another dog, write it down. The connection might not be that obvious and usually isn't. Catch anything that comes up even if it seems unrelated. After the current round, switch to the older memory. Tap on it just as you would the current one, breaking it down into specific emotions and pieces. Neutralize it. Then go back to the current event. Test it. If there's still intensity on any piece (or aspect), tap it down. If it feels neutral, you don't have to. Tapping on the earlier event has helped clear the current one.

Get experienced neutralizing several of these recent, but not traumatic, events. Then . . .

3. **Go Sherlock Holmes** You are seeing what EFT can do. The process is becoming more comfortable. You know where the points are and you've made a practice of feeling your feelings. But what about tapping for major life changes?

   - Define what you are looking to heal.
   - Set an intention to heal it.
   - Break down the big issue into very small, specific aspects.
   - Start tapping with how you feel about where you are right now, as it concerns the issue.
   - Follow the energy. This will be unique to each person. The energy will reveal where you need to go next in the tapping. Memories, beliefs, sensations, words you find yourself saying that carry a heavy charge, all of them are valuable clues. Be open to whatever comes up and tap on it.
   - Tap while asking yourself questions like:
     What does this remind me of?
     The last time I felt this way was _____

_____ (Fill in the blank with whatever pops up. There may be several responses to this. Allow them all and see which carry a charge. Tap repeatedly on the ones with a charge.)

- In some instances, you will need outside help. See Chapter 11.

4. **Feeling the Feelings Exercise . . . with Tapping** Maybe you're ready to hang up your Holmes hat because the investigative work hasn't uncovered much. Don't give up. You may be a feelings tapper.

Revisit that Feel the Feelings exercise from page 48–52. Do all the steps. As you experience the sensations, tap on them. You can gather more information about the sensations by asking yourself, and then answering, the following questions:

1. How big is this sensation?

2. Does the sensation have a shape? What shape is it?

3. What colors do I see?

4. What does this sensation sound like?

You may not have answers to all of these questions, but write down the ones you do get.

In the beginning, it may be easier to tap this exercise while describing the sensations out loud and doing the Set-Up and Reminders.

An example:

Set-Up: "Even though there's all this clenching tightness in my throat, I know I'll be okay."

Reminders: "this clenching," "this pain," "all this tightness," "tightness in my throat," "this feeling," "hard to swallow," "yellow," "big as a baseball." Use the details to help you focus on the energy.

Or:

> **Set-Up:** "Even though I feel red-hot swirling pain in my gut, I'm being present to this feeling."
>
> **Reminders:** "this red pain," "it's hot," "it's swirling," "I feel it right here in my gut," "this swirling, red pain."

After you've done this practice several times describing out loud what you are feeling, you may be able to do it without speaking at all.

1. Feel the sensations.

2. Focus on them.

3. Rate the intensity.

4. Tap while focusing on the sensations.

5. Check in to see what the sensations are doing. Follow and witness any changes.

6. Keep tapping until the energy dissipates completely.

What to Do If the Intensity Isn't Lessening

The basic EFT process I've shared with you does work. Seems simple, doesn't it? But simple is not always easy. Just making the effort to be present to current stress-inducing events can require effort. You're starting to view uncomfortable emotions in a very new way. Not as enemies to avoid, but rather information to be faced and energy to be cleared. It can be frustrating if the process doesn't seem to be clearing. Here's what to look for:

- **YOU MAY BE DEHYDRATED.** Drink a glass of water, then try again.

- **CHANGE SETTINGS.** Fluorescent lighting and EMFs can interfere. Try tapping in a different room or go outside.

- **YOU'RE NOT BEING SPECIFIC ENOUGH.** Write down the event and break it into the smallest possible pieces.

- **YOUR POLARITY IS REVERSED.** Do one or more of the exercises on pages 72 and 73 in this book.

- **YOU'RE HOMOLATERAL.** Do one or more of the exercises on pages 53 and 54.

- **YOU'RE TOO TIRED.** Energy clearing doesn't work well when you're tired. Releasing requires energy you may not have right now. Get rest and try again.

- **TAP ON SELF-JUDGMENTS.** You may need to tap on judgments you have about yourself for having the reaction or the problem. For example: With not getting a raise, you may believe this is because you're stupid. Tap on the self-judgment first: "Even though I'm stupid and it cost me the raise . . ." This usually allows the problem to clear.

- **FOCUS, FOCUS, AND MORE FOCUS.** EFT does require focus and it is very easy to switch to another aspect before the current one is cleared. This leaves you with several half-neutralized aspects and limited positive results. This can be a challenge for most newbie tappers. The more you focus, the easier it will be. And tapping on the feelings (sensations) rather than the story about what caused them can help tremendously.

- **GET HELP.** See Chapter 10, page 144.

TAPPING PRACTICES THAT WORK

The following are simple, step-by-step processes I've created that use tapping. They are easy and extremely powerful.

Releasing Practices and Creative Practices

When you want to create a fulfilling and enriching life, there are two different types of energy-healing practices to try.

First are **Releasing Practices**. These are processes that enable you to let go of painful memories, limiting beliefs, judgments about yourself and others, doubts, and fears. Those thoughts and feelings aren't just in your mind. They are actually in your body and energy field, clouding your light and negatively influencing your perception of life. All this old baggage feels awful and can get in the way of your happiness and success. The more of your energy that's tied up in the past, the less energy you have to make healthy changes in your life. Use Releasing Practices first to make internal space in your subconscious mind and energetic body for new ideas, nourishing beliefs, potent confidence, and expanded self-love.

Which brings me to **Creative Practices**. You may have heard of or even tried some of these practices before. They are very popular and used in everything from corporate business planning to sports psychology to personal development. When your energy is in alignment with these practices, they can be truly transformative. A few examples are:

1. Visualizing your desired life, or specific goal, as if it is happening right now.

2. Creating and repeating affirmations, which are statements in the present tense that reflect what you want to achieve. Example: I am healthy in every way.

3. Making lists of goals and following through on action steps to complete them.

4. Creating a vision board with photos of what you'd like to have and experience.

Creative practices get supercharged when combined with energy work.

Releasing Practice: The Tapping Forgiveness Practice

Humans. We can be messy, selfish, and disappointing at times, can't we? A happy life is one in which you are able to have nourishing relationships with others. But that can feel difficult or even impossible when you've been hurt or betrayed. And frankly, who *hasn't?* You may *want* to be open, to trust, to feel safe loving and being loved, and not understand what's blocking you. Forgiveness *is* the way out of these defensive patterns. But how?

Traditional forgiveness is to offer pardon or absolution to a person who has wronged you. You make a decision to "take the high road," to be a bigger person, and to let go of the anger or hurt that was created. This is always a healthy choice. Unresolved resentments are festering wounds that burden your outlook and weigh down your energy. I also firmly believe they negatively impact your health and keep you from moving forward. But if forgiveness is only taking place on the mental level, it can take a very long time to truly resolve, if it does at all. Forcing yourself to forgive and think loving thoughts about a person you were harmed by can feel impossible. And by resolved, I mean you no longer feel any pain when you think of the person and/or what he or she did.

Energetic forgiveness is very different. Allowing and then neutralizing the pain you've experienced comes first. All feelings of anger, resentment, grief, sadness, even hatred are welcomed, allowed, honored, expressed in a healthy way, and then freed through energy practices. When we approach forgiveness this way, how you feel about the person and your ability to let go of the wound are natural side effects of the release work. (See Changes in Perception, page 107.)

Signs You Need to Forgive

1. Life stopped after _____ happened (he left me, she humiliated me, they lied, I was robbed)

2. Your anger is spilling out over minor inconveniences (cashier gives you the wrong change, your friend forgot to call you back, the cat broke your vase)

3. You're repeating the same victim story over and over again (the divorce settlement, your sister got the ring in the will, that teacher who called you dumb)

4. Liver or gallbladder issues (the organs and meridians of anger, resentment, depression, and even guilt)

5. You avoid _____ (that person, mention of his/her name, things that remind you of him/her)

6. You're a person. In other words, absolutely everyone has something or someone to forgive. Forgiveness is not a practice done once. It becomes a regular practice for a healthy life. You do it for yourself, to free yourself from the pain of the past.

Forgiveness Works

Candice came to see me because her dating life was nonexistent. She was an educated and attractive woman in her mid-thirties with a successful marketing career she really enjoyed. Her company was made up of mostly male employees, many of whom were single and had similar interests. She traveled frequently for work and pleasure, often meeting new and interesting people. It didn't make sense! Her friends told her that men must find her intimidating. She tried online dating, but they'd fizzle out after a coffee or two. Candice became frustrated and a little hopeless. It was time to try something new. That meant energy coaching. As we tapped on her current disappointment, resentment from an earlier marriage came to the surface. Over the next few sessions, we cleaned it up, tapping on a major lie she had been told by her ex-husband and the memory of the moment she knew it was over. Then an earlier hurt emerged from age twelve, when her father had left her mother. We explored, tapped on, and neutralized the pain of that experience. After processing these painful events from her past, she was filled with a sense of peace she hadn't known before. She was able to forgive both her father and her ex-husband. Then she got it. On an energetic level, the pain and resentment from these unresolved wounds had been unconsciously sensed by any potential mates, thwarting her efforts to fall in love again. Within weeks, she met a new man and was able to move forward in her romantic life.

The following is one of my favorite processes because it is a big life-changer. I still use this myself whenever needed.

THE TAPPING FORGIVENESS PRACTICE: STEP-BY-STEP

Supplies: Pen and paper or a journal. Think practical versus fancy. Write by hand whenever possible. Privacy is a must.

1. **Identify a person you want to forgive.** When doing this for the first time, it's easier to pick someone who has recently hurt or angered you. The energy of that emotion will be fresh and easier to access. After you've done the process a few times and felt the results, then consider "the biggies": mom, dad, biological parents, grandparents, siblings, former lovers and

spouses, children, bosses, teachers, coaches ... you get the idea. If you have experienced a serious trauma, work on this process with a qualified mental health professional. (See Chapter 10, page 144.)

2. **Identify the situation that harmed you.** If you're starting with a recent experience, there may be only one. If you've experienced multiple hurts with this same person, start with the most recent and focus on that one only. Once neutralized, you can repeat this process with other memories.

3. **Identify the emotion(s) you're feeling.** Some possibilities to consider: anger, rage, resentment, frustration, guilt, fear, anxiety, terror, panic, shock, disappointment, hurt, sadness, heartbreak, grief, depression, confusion, humiliation, disgust, shame, abandonment, betrayal, worthlessness, insecurity, and annoyance.

4. **Writing About—Exercise #1** This is your chance to tell the story of what happened.

   Begin writing in a stream-of-consciousness fashion. Put pen to paper and express without ceasing, allowing your conscious and then subconscious mind to unload. If you think you've run out of material to spew, write "I don't know what to write" over and over again until something else comes through. You've likely been running this story on your "mental treadmill" anyway; now you're giving it a place to land: all the gory details and supporting evidence for how wrong, wrong, wrong it all was. This isn't your college admission essay. It's a healing exercise. No one will see it but you. There's no witness to your terrible spelling, penmanship, and grammar.

   Get messy!

5. **Writing To*—Exercise #2** This is your chance to tell that person off, say what you need to say, get "revenge," and express without censoring.

*This letter is for your eyes only. *Do not send it* for two very important reasons:

a) If you write the letter with the intention of the person reading it, you will not be completely honest, raw, and real. This defeats the purpose of the exercise.

b) When the exercise is done effectively, you won't feel the same way afterward. You'll likely regret having sent it.

Write a letter to this person. If you could say anything at all, without repercussions, without being mature, ethical, or kind, what would you say? Why are you upset? Say it here. Be as nasty as you want. Swear! Threaten revenge! Demean! Insult! Allow your human animal nature to ooze onto the page. Allow it all without judgment.

Get toxic!

And don't stop until you've completely emptied out.

A note for Spiritual Types, Moral Mavens, and the Big Hearted: This exercise may be challenging in the beginning. You are kind and compassionate, at times to a fault, and strive hard to be a good person. You may believe these thoughts and feelings are wrong and harmful. You may feel guilty for even having them. Start there. Get *those* feelings out onto the page first, then allow what's underneath.

What you suppress will cause you stress. What you deny will crucify. (You get the point.) Emotions are not logical. They are not good or bad. They are simply information. And once the full spectrum of them is allowed without judgment, you will be freed. I promise you.

This is a healthy place for these thoughts and feelings to land, while helping you immensely and without harming anyone else.

A new definition to consider: Good people are ones who use healthy outlets for emotional expression; therefore these feelings don't harm anyone, including themselves.

6. **Read Writing About Exercise #1 out loud.** Then close your eyes and feel what's happening in your body. Give it an intensity rating from 1 to 10.

7. **TAP. Read the exercise out loud and tap through the points.** Be sure to take a few deep breaths between rounds. Recheck the intensity. Keep going until you get to a 0 or 1. If a specific memory from the past rises to the surface, capture it by writing it down.

8. **Read Writing To Exercise #2 out loud.** Then close your eyes and feel what's happening in your body. Give it an intensity rating from 1 to 10.

9. **Tap again. Read the exercise out loud and tap through the points.** Be sure to take a few deep breaths between rounds. Recheck the intensity. Keep going until you get to a 0 or 1. If a specific memory from the past rises to the surface, capture it by writing it down.

10. **Test.** Return to the original offense. Repeat the memory in your mind. It will likely appear fuzzy, unclear, or simply less important. If there's still uncomfortable emotion, get tapping again.

11. **Now forgive.** If you already have a religious or spiritual practice of forgiveness, use that. If you don't, here are a few you can try:

Close your eyes, imagine the person standing in front of you, and say to them (silently or out loud), "I choose my freedom and I let this old energy go easily, fully, and completely."

Go to a river. Pick up something natural in the setting, like a leaf or twig. Hold it to your chest and imagine the energy of that situation and person moving into the stick. Toss it into the river and say "I let this go. I allow healing. I am free."

If this is a person you still have a relationship with, imagine them in front of you and a brightly lit cord in between you that grows and covers you both completely. Intend that any remaining discord be absorbed by the light.

Tap through the points saying "I completely forgive you, _____ (person's name)" and "I'm willing and able to let this go completely."

A FEW FINAL NOTES

This is a complete process but you can take out the pieces that resonate with you. All steps may not be needed each time. The keys are to **freely express then neutralize those feelings with tapping.**

An audio option: If you're an auditory learner, experiment with recording the writing exercises instead. Use an app on your phone or program on your computer. Then let it rip! Listen to the recording and tap along. Stop the recording at any moments of intensity and repeat what you said over and over again, resuming when you feel a shift. Do as many times as needed until you reach relief.

Creative Practice: Visualizing a Goal

Pick a goal you'd like to achieve.

Vision Boards That Work

Back when I first learned to do these, there was no Internet. I would get a big piece of poster board and cut out pictures from magazines. Now, with a two-second image search, you can find pictures of absolutely everything online. There are even apps and programs for creating phone or computer versions, no glue needed.

Go old-school and print, or go with the digital versions. The best type of vision board is the one you will actually follow through on and create. A vision board thought about isn't one that will work. You need to see it. If you're an artsy/crafty type and will enjoy the process of creating the paper version, then go for it. The advantage is you can make it as big as you want. It's not limited to screen size. If you're limited on time or just really comfortable with technology, then explore the online versions. Or open a blank word processing document and use that.

Making a Vision Board

1. Use photos/images for each area of your life. We've talked a lot in this book about creating balance. Make a balanced board that represents a balanced life.

   AREAS TO INCLUDE:
   Health
   Career
   Money/material things
   Relationships
   Family
   Home/vehicle

Hobbies/creative pursuits (travel, etc.)

Spiritual life

2. Group photos for specific life areas together. Arrange in a circle, if possible, with spiritual pictures in the center.

3. Make it eye appealing. Include colors, phrases, and designs that you love. This way you'll *want* to look at it.

4. Hang it somewhere private and look at daily. Or visit the digital version once a day.

Now for the fun part.

How to Tap on Your Vision Board

Tapping with a Vision Board Using Feelings

Look at it. Look at the images. Take them in. Then choose one area to focus on.

1. **Close your eyes.** What feelings in your body did the images inspire? Scan the body, feeling for areas of tightness or twinges of discomfort.

2. **Tap on those sensations.** Just like in previous exercises, be present to what is, feel the feelings, ask questions, and describe those sensations. Tap until all discomfort is resolved.

3. **Test.** Look at the images again. See if there's any unpleasant reaction. Make sure all discomfort is gone.

4. **Look at the images again.** Breathe in and out through the center of the chest for a minute or two. Imagine what it would feel like to have that item, job, person, or experience in your life. See yourself having it until you feel warm, positive feelings.

5. **Tap on the positive feelings.** Set an intention to expand the positive sensation as you silently tap through the points. Or choose one point you like and tap on that one.

6. **Move on to a second area.** Or revisit it another day. Tap until you only have good feelings when you look at the vision board.

Tapping with a Vision Board Using Thoughts

1. **Look at it.** Look at the images. Take them in. Then choose one area to focus on.

2. **Close your eyes or leave them open (your choice).** What limiting thoughts come to mind? "That's impossible." "That will never happen for me."

3. **Tap on those thoughts.** Tap on the statement or statements until all discomfort is resolved.

4. **Test.** See if there are any additional limiting thoughts. Make sure all discomfort is gone.

5. **Look at the images again.** Breathe in and out through the center of the chest for a minute or two. Imagine what it would feel like to have that item, job, person, or experience in your life. See yourself having it until supportive thoughts come up. "I can have this." "I deserve this." "This is possible."

6. **Tap on the positive thoughts.** Say the positive statements out loud as you tap through the points. Or choose one point you like and tap on that one.

7. **Move on to a second area.** Or revisit it another day. Tap until you only have good thoughts when you look at the vision board.

9

MAKING YOUR PRACTICE A PART OF YOUR LIFE

I recently got a familiar email. It was from my new client, Lana. She said, "I'm working these practices and doing my homework. I'm releasing what comes up. At least it feels like I'm doing it right. Then I get this awesome sense of calm. I've been wanting to feel like this for my whole life. But within days, it's gone. My boyfriend calls and says something stupid and I'm back in that stress place. It never ends!"

Welcome to energy healing, my dear readers. Hang in there. It will all be worth it. I promise.

This email is familiar because it's what I hear from anyone who makes energy healing practices a part of their life. I call it the Plates at the Buffet Effect. You hit the buffet restaurant and grab the plate that's on top, ready to fill it. But as soon as it's in your hands, the next plate pops up. How wonderful for the person behind you. But if the plate you're holding was that painful childhood event you're resolving, you may not be so thrilled when life presents you with your next healing assignment.

The subconscious mind knows good stuff is happening. You're weeding your inner garden. Old gunk is going bye-bye. It thinks you need some further encouragement and would like to help. It's like you're loading the dishwasher and your child comes up behind you with a big tray of dirty dishes from his bedroom and says, "Hey, while you're doing that, I thought I'd bring you these." Gee, thanks.

Let me say this right now: you will never be finished. As long as you're alive, walking around in that body of yours, and taking classes at Earth School, you will have baggage to release, energy to balance, things to learn, areas of growth to unfold, and people to forgive. *I know.* What a downer! I wasn't so thrilled with the news myself when I first learned it. I had studied with a powerful shaman named Christina Pratt. She once said to me, "Everyone I know is complaining about having to heal. 'It's so much work!' What do you think we're here for? This is what we came to do." I've since learned she was absolutely right.

Life *does* get better. A whole lot better. You do heal. At times in astounding ways. At times in subtle ways. Anything and everything can change. And then does. You feel better and better and better. Until you don't. Until a new problem surfaces. "Here we go again." Then you heal. Again. There's that peace. Sure do love that feeling!

It happens in cycles. When the going gets tough, don't jump off the path. Keep going. There's another big breakthrough up ahead. Followed by calm. Then another damn (blessed) growth opportunity. Just. Keep. Going.

When you begin to see how easily you can heal, how much you can change, how much better life can get, you may be inspired to dive in headfirst. "I'll just tap on every bad thing that ever happened to me and within two months I'll be done, a brand-new person."

You can actually approach your healing in a methodical way like this with EFT. Gary Craig called it the Personal Peace Procedure. You list one hundred specific events you wish never happened to you, then give each an intensity rating. You pick the most intense events to start with, tapping on and neutralizing one per day. I know many people for whom this was a life-changing experience. If this sounds appealing, do an Internet search for "Personal Peace Procedure" and you'll find a variety of resources and approaches. You can achieve that brand-new-person feeling. You're off to an amazing start. (Just know there will be more. There's always more.)

I also know people who've tried this procedure a few different ways and times, but it didn't seem to work for them. The process felt forced. They couldn't access the feelings for many of the events (and all the bound-up energy along with it). It didn't create the experience of lasting peace that they hoped for.

There's no right or wrong here. There's what works. There's what doesn't work. Work what works for you always. Don't waste time on anything you aren't benefitting from. There's always another approach. I offer you an alternative approach that works well for me and many others.

For myself, I like to take a more organic method in my healing. Life always seems to bring me what I most need to work on. When I'm awake and aware, I have those moments where I say, "Ah, here's another one. Let's do this!" I've come to actually welcome these healing opportunities.

A couple of years ago, I was driving to my church. We were putting on a production of *The Vagina Monologues*. (If you're not aware of this play, each winter women all over the world perform the same series of monologues. One hundred percent of all ticket sales collected are donated to nonprofits that support women and girls who've experienced violence.) I was driving to our dress rehearsal. Just as I rounded the corner and slowly began pulling into the parking lot, I was hit hard from behind by another car. There had been people crossing on foot in front of my car, and thankfully they jumped out of the way as my car lurched forward. I had been hit by a teen driver who was texting. I wasn't hurt beyond the normal whiplash and body tension, but I still exploded with tears and felt inconsolable for much of the evening. I limped through my performance, forgetting several lines, and the director wondered how I was going to get through the next three days. She wasn't the only one wondering! While I watched the other performers, I immediately began cooling Triple Heater, grounding my energy, and patting my body down. Later, at home, I began to tap on the accident. Very quickly, a memory surfaced. I was eight, in the back of my dad's car when it was hit from behind. We were on the way to our church for my first-communion rehearsal. A car accident. On the way to church. For a rehearsal. The similarities were staggering. The memory held several specific events. The accident itself. The police coming. Being put in the back of a police car so the officer could drop me off at church while my father stayed with the car. The reaction of people at the church when I told them what happened. I tapped through it all. And even though I felt like I got hit by a bus the next day, I was still able to act, and act well, in all three performances. I didn't forget a single word. The current event had brought up all that old emotion and energy from the past to the surface. Because it was right in my face, I was able to heal it quickly.

FACING THE PLATE ON TOP: CATCHING THE NEXT WAVE

Your brilliant subconscious mind has a very specific order for what it brings you in your healing. That order will likely not make sense to you. I spend a lot of time examining this for my clients and myself. It still doesn't always make sense to me either! It's not chronological. It doesn't even go from worst to least or easiest to hardest. But there *is* a rhythm and wisdom to it.

Rather than delve into the depth of your past, I'd like to offer another approach. Consider making your life your practice. Face the plate on top. What happened today, yesterday, or last week that still stings as you think about it? You'll know it needs to be addressed if your emotional reaction is out of context with the situation. If it happened a day ago and you're still thinking about it, there's likely a healing opportunity present.

Penelope was the angriest client I had ever worked with. There wasn't much that *didn't* set her off. One day she arrived for her online session fuming over an exchange she had had with a pharmacist. Penelope had a question about a prescription medication she was taking and asked the pharmacist for information; he answered her, but in a way that she felt was dismissive. It had been a week and she was still enraged over it. She had called customer service and was about to write a letter, asking for the pharmacist to be fired. The intensity of the reaction was completely out of proportion to what had happened. I knew there was healing gold under this seemingly innocent incident. As we tapped, Penelope remembered a time her older sister had humiliated her. Her teen sister had been spending time in the family room with her boyfriend. Penelope kept interrupting them, asking questions, as little sisters can tend to do. Finally, her sister said, "Only an idiot would ask that!" which embarrassed her in front of the guest. And now, in the present time, her sister was coming for a visit in a few days. The situation with the pharmacist brought it all back and we were able to release long-held pain. As a bonus, Penelope and her sister ended up having the best visit they'd ever shared. She said to me, "We're not the same people we were as kids. We're different now." With energy no longer stuck in the past, she had a change in perspective.

You've been practicing feeling your feelings. You've worked on being more conscious, more aware. You've felt how quickly you can calm yourself. This is where it pays off. Instead of ignoring, avoiding, and distracting yourself from upsetting situations, you can now catch them. "Uh oh, my heart is racing. There's that stomach clenching again. My mind just won't let this damn thing go! Yikes! This feeling is frighteningly familiar. Here we go again." Make a commitment to face whatever is presenting itself and resolve it. It's happening now for a reason. You may not know what that reason is, but trust that this may, in fact, be the best time to address it. Do what you are able to do to let the pain from the past go. Bring calm and sanity back to your nervous system and your mind.

DAILY SITUATIONS AND HOW TO SHIFT THEM: A PRACTICE

We lead such busy lives that the temptation to put off clearing and balancing is always looming. "Maybe this weekend," you think, but then forget once the free time arrives, if it arrives at all.

When you clear and balance on a regular basis, you will be

amazed at the changes you experience. Having a regular practice to follow can help. It may very well prevent the major emotional crashes that happen when we've forgotten to practice.

A Sample Daily Practice

- **When you wake up,** before getting out of bed, tap vigorously on the collarbone points. This is your inner furnace. Imagine stoking that fire you will need to get through the day. (1 minute)

- **While taking a shower,** balance your polarity. Get your energy running in the right direction. (30 seconds to 1 minute)

- **Rub and slap the bottoms of your feet,** to get grounded, before putting on your shoes. (30 seconds to 1 minute)

- **Shield up** before you leave your home. Clear your body with light. Then bubble yourself, your loved ones (including pets), your home, and your car. (2 to 5 minutes)

- **Set an intention for the kind of day you'd like to have.** (30 seconds to 1 minute)

- **If you drive to work,** tap the side of your hand on the steering wheel. At a stoplight, do a round of tapping through the rest of the points. (Variable, but won't lengthen your commute)

- **If you take public transportation,** do the finger and wrist holds. (3 minutes)

- **Calm Triple Heater** prior to working by pressing the gamut point on the back of the hand and consciously breathing in through the nose and out through the mouth. Can also be done before or during a meeting. (2 minutes)

- **Got triggers?** (Who doesn't?) Go to the office restroom. Think of what triggered you. Feel the sensations in your body. Do a few rounds of silent tapping. (5 minutes)

If any major events come up or it doesn't feel complete, make a note to yourself to clean it up later.

- **Shush your nervous system** before lunch. (30 seconds to 1 minute)

- **Shush your nervous system** after lunch. (30 seconds to 1 minute)

- **3:00 P.M. slump?** Thump your collarbone and thymus points. You may not need that coffee after all. (30 seconds to 1 minute)

- **Balance your polarity** again for the commute home. (30 seconds to 1 minute)

- **Clear the day.** Set a timer for ten minutes and tap on whatever irked you that day. Speak out loud here, really loud if you need to, and just let it flow. If you're tempted to vent to a household member, go for it! Just tap the entire time you're doing it. Trust me, they'll stop giggling after you've done it the first time. Maybe you'll even be able to encourage them to tap along with you. (10 minutes)

- **Calm Triple Heater** before bed. (5 minutes max)

Thirty-eight minutes maximum, spread throughout the day, mostly while you are already occupied with other mandatory activities. You're doing them anyway. Get some healing in! You've been clearing and balancing all day. The power in this is you're paying attention to your energy at several small intervals. And those tiny check-ins and practices can make a big difference in how you feel. You'll start building confidence in your healing and remember a shift is only a moment away.

OWN YOUR JOURNEY

We can get used to turning over control of our health and happiness to other people. Not to get all Dr. Phil on you, but how's that working for you? Even with the best-trained, ethical, experienced, kind, and resourceful health professionals, they still are not *you*. They aren't living in your energy field. They see your imbalances through the filters of their modalities and belief systems.

Sara came to me in utter frustration and confusion. She'd broken out in itchy painful rashes on her legs and nothing had helped. Her doctor suspected an allergy and prescribed an antihistamine, but it didn't make a difference. Her herbalist thought it was an overgrowth of candida that was the cause. She had Sara make strict dietary changes and go on a regimen of candida-killing supplements. The rashes remained. Her therapist felt it was the result of her deep-seated self-consciousness. After all, with the rashes, she had an excuse to cover up and avoid being seen. But this intriguing perspective didn't reduce the symptoms either. By the time she came to me, she said, "I don't know what to think! What's causing this?" I could see why she felt frustrated. I told her, "Each of these competent professionals is seeing your symptom through the lens of what each does. The doctor treats allergies. So, he sees an allergic response. The herbalist is well educated on candida, so she sees an overgrowth. The therapist looks at it from a mental point of view. And I'm an energy coach. I will see this as an energy imbalance. That's what I'm trained to do." This wasn't what she wanted to hear. She was hoping I had "the answer." And that's understandable because, after all, she was in pain. Even though I didn't know the answer, I knew her energy had had it all along. We started by tapping on the itchiness and the pain. Then tremendous anger came up. Her husband had taken a promotion without consulting her. It meant he'd be away from home even more than he already had been. Eureka! The rash began to clear almost immediately. She returned to the herbalist to get a salve to help soothe the skin. Within two weeks, the skin on her legs was healthy. She had had the answers all along.

Getting answers doesn't always happen that easily or that quickly. (If only!) But just knowing the answers are within you can bring you great peace along with the motivation to keep going until you figure it out. And you'll be less tempted to give away your own inner authority. You will come to love owning your healing journey.

You Don't Have to Be a Hero

Yes, you need to own your healing practice. You're the only one who can. But you don't have to be a hero. It's not wise to handle everything on your own. There are always very good reasons to get outside help, which you'll learn about in the next chapter.

10

GETTING HELP

WHEN TO GET HELP FROM A QUALIFIED PROFESSIONAL

Doctors don't perform their own surgeries. Dentists don't pull their own teeth. There's a time for self-practice and there's a time for professional help. Every top energy healer I know uses a coach or practitioner for their own major blocks.

Here's how to know when it's time to call a practitioner.

- **You're not improving on your own.** This is very common. Rather than getting discouraged and giving up, be open to giving a professional a try. Energy healing modalities can take minutes to learn and yet a lifetime to master. Sometimes it can be difficult to do focused work that actually makes a difference. We often start working on our "big issues" rather than using energy healing for everyday stressors. It's like getting behind the wheel of a Maserati before we've mastered the tricycle. Start small and bring the biggies to someone well trained in working with them.

- **You've experienced a trauma.** It's hard to find someone who *hasn't* experienced a trauma. A few examples of the countless small traumas anyone can have: getting fired, a minor car accident, being stood up on a date, falling out of a tree, or being gossiped about. The Big Ones we normally associate with trauma are physical, emotional, or sexual abuse; being a victim of or witnessing a crime; going through a war; being abandoned as a child; giving up a baby for adoption; or moving to a new country.

  Here's a very important point to consider: *how* a person responds to a potentially traumatic situation is highly individual. Sensitive people and those with over-reactive nervous systems can feel traumatized over what another would consider a normal day at the office. Personality and innate temperament also influence how one is affected energetically. What is minor or major trauma will depend on how it has affected that person. I see this when working with children in the same family who are experiencing an identical change, like their parents divorcing. One child may be deeply wounded by this while another is moving through the changes with ease. If it feels traumatic for you, it *is* a trauma. Don't judge your own experiences by what happened. If it felt bad, it was bad.

  Here's a few signs your trauma needs professional help:

  You haven't felt the same since _____(the divorce, 9/11, child left home).

You feel numb or terrified at the idea of addressing it.

You believe life would have been different if it hadn't been for _____ (that attack, the bullying, that divorce).

You carry great shame about it.

You're experiencing a phobia and don't know the underlying cause

The idea of working on yourself is too frightening.

Sometimes the smartest choice we can make is to call on a professional who is experienced in trauma work and get the right help.

■ **You've been diagnosed with a mental or physical illness (or suspect you have one).** Energy healing is not a substitute for professional therapeutic care. It can be a highly effective complement to traditional allopathic or alternative treatment. If you've received a diagnosis, get good support from a licensed health practitioner or mental health specialist. Then enlist the support of a qualified energy professional to be on your healing team. Energy healers make time for emotional support that busy doctors don't always have. Some licensed mental health professionals also do energy work as part of their practice. The key is to get help so you can then better help yourself.

■ **You're not physically able to work on yourself.** You're too tired, have mobility issues, you're struggling with chronic illness, or you're simply too busy or burned-out to learn how to do this for yourself. Finding someone you trust and enlisting their care is a good idea. Ultimately, you are your own best advocate and healer. No one knows you and your energy system better than you do. Approach seeing a professional practitioner as a way to ease your current struggles, access more energy, and get you started on a path to well-being. Once the healing has started and you're feeling better, it will be easier to work on yourself. You get to keep the momentum going rather than get it started yourself.

- **You're an overthinking, overlearning, workshop/self-help junkie, yet having trouble doing practices for yourself.** Let me just start by saying, this is something I truly understand. I spent six years learning EFT with multiple classes, workshops, books, and newsletters. I completely immersed myself in the knowledge of it. But I was only actually tapping about monthly, not daily as I do now. To feel the magnitude of what energy healing can do, you have to do more than just read about it. You must experience it! So much of what shifts is beyond the level of regular, everyday thinking. It was when I finally started working with an EFT practitioner on my own issues that I truly understood what this work can do. This led me to becoming a practitioner for others. I'm now in my tenth year of professional practice and I'm still learning; it's a lifelong commitment. But as I'm researching, I am also practicing what I am learning on myself and with others. I have enriching partnerships with other practitioners where we work and learn together.

Work with a professional to get out of your head and into your energetic responses. You might be surprised where it could lead you!

CHOOSING THE RIGHT PRACTITIONER

- **Get a referral from someone you know.** People can be shy about this. "What will they think if I'm looking for an energy healer?" You'd be surprised that this work is often a well-kept secret.

When I tell people what I do, the most common reaction is curiosity and interest. Then come the True Confessions. "I saw someone who balanced my chakras after a breakup" is whispered conspiratorially. "My sister tapped with me after I'd argued with my son and it really helped" is shared when no one is looking. It's time to let go of the stigma!

But if you don't want to ask someone you know, social media is a good place to start. Find Facebook groups (search under "EFT," "energy medicine," and "energy healing") and describe what you're looking for. Some practitioners offer a free getting-to-know-you session so you can see if you're an ideal fit.

- **Ask about:**

    Educational and career background

    Hours and type(s) of training(s)

    Years in practice

    Specialties

    If they have a mentor or coach, or undergo supervision

    If they use the services of a coach or practitioner for their own issues (Look for a yes on this!)

    If they have a certification or license (if so, from where?)

    What a typical session entails

    Their thoughts on ethics (listen for the word "confidentiality")

    Answers to the above are a good start.

- **Get a feel for rapport.** But don't underestimate the often intangible qualities of rapport that can be difficult to define. A feeling of connection with a potential practitioner is important. Most often my clients report that they just "knew" (got an intuitive hit) that I was the person to work with. A practitioner making you feel safe and heard can be even more important than the number of years they've been in practice. Use your head but also consult your heart.

- **Ask the practitioner for references from past or current clients.** Keep in mind, practitioners are only going to give contact information for people who've enjoyed their services. So, when you follow up, have specific questions ready, like:

> How long did you work with him or her?
> What changes did you experience?
> How did the work make you feel?
> What do you like best and least about him or her?
> Do you believe they practiced confidentiality?

If you have any concerns, share them with the reference, if they seem open. They may have had your same worries and can put you at ease.

Check out their websites. Read their blogs. Then google them. Just because a practitioner writes interesting articles and has a devoted following does not necessarily mean they are an effective healer. It may just mean they're a good marketer. While great for business and an admirable quality in its own right, this doesn't *always* translate into deep, transformative work. Look on their websites and social media for what I call improbable promises. These sound like "My coaching will give you the perfect life!" or "I can fix your problem in three easy sessions!" If they are guaranteeing something that can't possibly be guaranteed, that's a red flag. I've studied personal growth and healing for three decades and there is still a great mystery about it. I've seen and personally experienced what can only be described as miracles. And there are times I've had to work, practice, and heal for months or years to experience the kind of shift I wanted. While the promise of a quick, easy fix can be very seductive, know that healing is a process. Work with someone who is honest about that.

Be sure to google them and see what other information about them is available. You may learn exactly what you need to hire them or move on.

{ 11 }

WHAT'S DIVINE LOVE GOT TO DO WITH IT?

Throughout this book, I write about this potent, powerful force that is the creative medium in all "stuff," including us, and how we can feel it and work with it. This stuff is called energy, which you now know goes by many different names. I focused on the numerous physical and emotional benefits.

Energy work is completely secular in nature and you do not need to have any spiritual beliefs whatsoever to use these practices. Energy healing is done by people of all faiths and people with no faith whatsoever. Simply practice what you've learned as outlined in previous chapters. You can skip ahead to the book's conclusion.

But if you are a spiritual person or just curious, I'm going to give you another benefit. There are spiritual enhancements that come from balanced energy.

No matter what your religious and/or spiritual beliefs and practices, energy healing practices can enhance them.

PRAYER

Maybe you've recently lost your job or are struggling with a stubborn health challenge. Or you've heard about a terrifying tragedy on the news and it has you feeling lost and uncertain. Far too often, we go it alone, trying to solve our problems or calm ourselves without asking for divine help.

I am a firm believer in the power of prayer. In fact, I pray with my open coaching clients and they often report it's their favorite part of the session. It's a spiritual way of aligning our energy and inviting forth something greater to set transformation into motion.

Prayer is a powerful way to:

- feel connected
- get a positive start to the day or turn one around that's going in the wrong direction
- send love and healing intentions to others
- become fully present
- invite forth miracles and blessings

It seems to be human nature to first try to fix everything yourself, *then* turn to the higher power or deity of your understanding when you haven't gotten far. What if you *started* by asking for help?

Often when we pray, it's from a place of worry or fear. Getting calm before and during prayer can allow you to feel the energy of your higher power.

Let's look at two types of prayer.

Asking Prayer

This is what you most often think of with prayer. It usually goes something like this:

"Dear God, please help me be a better person and to forgive my boss for that insulting comment she said yesterday. I'd also really like to have a good day today. Keep me and my children safe. I love You. Amen."

When saying this type of prayer, try your hands in the following positions:

1. Traditional palm-to-palm position, with the thumbs pressed firmly against the sternum. You'll be stimulating the conception vessel, one of the two major energy vessels in Traditional Chinese Medicine.

2. Traditional palm-to-palm position, placing the thumbs against the top of the bridge of the nose, in between the eyebrows and in the center of the forehead. This center of the forehead point is called the brow chakra and more commonly referred to as the Third Eye. You'll be stimulating this energy center of solutions and be pressing on the EFT eyebrow points as well.

3. One hand on top of the other placed on the center of the chest.

Using one of these methods will bring calm and clarity, allowing you to access solutions as you pray.

Affirmations or Affirmative Prayer

Affirmations are statements about a desired feeling or experience, stated in the present tense.

A few examples:

I am living in the perfect house for me.

I feel at ease wherever I go.

Life is working perfectly for me in every experience.

Affirmative prayer is a method for creating a prayer from a series of affirmations. Instead of asking your higher power, you state it as if it's already been answered.

An example:

"Thank you, God, for making me a better person each and every day. Thank you for leading my thoughts and feelings in forgiving my boss and creating a great day for me. I appreciate You protecting me and my children always. I am blessed. Amen."

For affirmations to be effective, they need to be believable. That's what can make them hard to do.

Tap on any doubts you may have and then pray or say your affirmations. See also the vision board exercise on page 131 for more information.

Energy Movement During Prayer or Meditation

During any type of prayer or meditation, here's a movement you can do that feels calming and connecting.

Place your hand out in front of you and trace a figure eight or infinity pattern in the air, over and over again. Trace these symbols on your body and off to the sides. Imagine you are drawing these patterns all around you.

This movement is also an all-over energy balancer and stress reliever.

Balance your energy during your religious and/or spiritual practices, including this infinity symbol exercise, or any of the others shared previously in the book. You may experience a more profound sense of connection or deeper feelings of peace and tranquility. Meditators find it helps quiet the mental chatter and they can reach the space between the thoughts more readily. Most of all, combining energy practices with spiritual ones helps you to be more present. These practices don't just use your mind. Now your whole body and energy field are involved in the process. So often we aren't fully in the present moment, even when we are praying or meditating. It's so easy to get distracted, lose focus, and be right back in our everyday thinking. When you are fully present, you get to experience the benefits in real time, in the only moment we really have, this one.

This is also an area where you can get creative.

If you do yoga, what can you use from this book before your practice? Could you tap on the pain in your tight hamstrings? Or balance your polarity so your practice flows more easily?

Or if you're walking a labyrinth, how about taking off your shoes and taking each step consciously?

Whatever you do to experience your spiritual life, energy healing practices can enhance it. Particularly if you've been doing the same practices for years, energy healing can bring a renewed freshness and awareness. Be open to experimenting and let yourself be surprised.

CONCLUSION: NOW WHAT?

Learning anything new can feel daunting at times. Here you've had this energy body for your whole life and only now learning you can work with it, creating positive changes in your life. No one had ever told you that before!

When starting, it can feel like you're all thumbs. "Wait, where do my fingers tap again? How is this supposed to feel? Am I doing this right??" The temptation can be to get lost in study and perfectionism, waiting to run before you've even crawled.

Energy healing *does* work. When you work it. So, please, WORK IT!

If I have any regrets, it's that in the beginning I spent too much time studying energy healing and not enough time actually practicing it. In all my earnestness, I wanted to get it right! I was so worried about getting it wrong! But the truth is, your energy field is very forgiving. There's not much you can get wrong. As you work with it, listen to it, be with it, and start to give it what it needs, it will teach you what no one else can. Including me.

Consider me your Energy Concierge. I was here to introduce, to make connections, show you what's possible, and break it down so it can be easy. Instead of front-row seats to *Hamilton*, I'm giving you the ticket out of your lifelong anxiety. Or endless exhaustion. Or debilitating grief.

The practices I've shared are a start, a tip, a tidbit, a sampling. You may decide to go deeper: read other books, take live classes, find a mentor, and meet others in the field. This would thrill me! If I've started a fire within you, then that makes me very honored indeed. Follow that passion and trust where it takes you. Be sure to check out the Resources section that follows.

And know that you could take the practices and principles shared here and work with them for years, never getting bored, never needing another lesson. Sometimes the simplest practices, when thoroughly owned, end up being the most profound. Allow them to teach you. If you have an inkling to switch or alter an aspect, do it. Get creative with your practice. Then measure the results. Use the information here to master the color wheel. Then go on to paint your masterpieces. This book is here for you to return to, again and again, as a resource and a guide.

BEGIN ANYWHERE. BUT *DO* BEGIN.

The best way to create a new habit is to couple it with one you already have. Since I was a small child, I've always watched an hour of TV or a movie before bed. It isn't the healthiest of habits, but not one I'm invested in changing at this time. So, I do energy balancing exercises while I watch, turning a rather useless habit into a helpful one. I balance my polarity and calm Triple Heater, paving the way for restful sleep. If I'm watching anything frightening or sad, I tap so I'm not creating those feelings within myself. Think about something you're already doing. If you go to the gym, spend a few minutes crossing over before your workout. If you meditate, tap for a couple minutes on your mental chatter first. Find ways to incorporate a few of these practices into your everyday life. Don't wait until you have a few free hours to get immersed. Use the Quick Tips. Just use them consciously. See how you feel before, during, and after. Let yourself be amazed at how easy it is to feel better.

The more you practice, the better you will feel. The better you feel, the more you'll want to practice. A day will come when you will wonder how you had managed so well without this knowledge. Then you'll remember how hard "managing" was. And maybe it hadn't gone so well after all. You may even have a few happy results to report. That chronic upset stomach healed. That workplace anxiety gone. That troubling relationship transformed. Yes, all of this *is* possible. Not just for me and my tribe of healing professionals. Not just for the clients we see. Healing is equally available for every single person on this planet.

And, yes. This does include you.

Listen. Be open. Practice. Feel.

Allow your balanced energy to lead you into a more magnificent life. It awaits.

Know I'm rooting for you all the way.

RESOURCES

Acupuncture and Traditional Chinese Medicine

OVERVIEW BOOKS

The Web That Has No Weaver: Understanding Chinese Medicine, by Ted J. Kaptchuk

Between Heaven and Earth: A Guide to Chinese Medicine, by Harriet Beinfield and Efrem Korngold

Acupressure (see also Acupuncture)

BOOK

Acupressure's Potent Points: A Guide to Self-Care for Common Ailments, by Michael Reed Gach

Brennan Healing Science/Brennan Integration Work

OFFICIAL WEBSITE

www.barbarabrennan.com

BOOKS

Hands of Light: A Guide to Healing Through the Human Energy Field, by Barbara Ann Brennan

Core Light Healing: My Personal Journey and Advanced Healing Concepts for Creating the Life You Long to Live, by Barbara Ann Brennan

Cranial Sacral Therapy and Massage

WEBSITE THAT SUPPORTS PRACTITIONERS, STUDENTS, AND SCHOOLS

www.craniosacraltherapy.org

WEBPAGE FOR A BEGINNER'S GUIDE

www.cranialtherapycentre.com/a-beginners-guide-to-craniosacral -therapy/

BOOKS

Harmonizing Your Craniosacral System: Self-Treatments for Improving Your Health By Daniel Agustoni

Craniosacral Therapy and the Energetic Body: An Overview of Craniosacral Biodynamics By Roger Gilchrist

Emotional Freedom Techniques (EFT or Tapping)

GOLD STANDARD EFT TAPPING TRAINING

General information and training materials from creator Gary Craig:

www.emofree.com

AAMET INTERNATIONAL

(ASSOCIATION FOR THE ADVANCEMENT OF MERIDIAN ENERGY TECHNIQUES)

For excellent EFT trainings and certification information: https://aametinternational.org/

TAPPING Q&A PODCAST

Free, high-quality tapping podcasts from host Gene Monterastelli with a variety of other experts:

http://tappingqanda.com/category/podcast/

EFT UNIVERSE

Thousands of EFT articles and case studies: www.eftuniverse.com /faqs/eft-and-tapping-hundreds-of-case-studies

EFT BOOK FOR NEWBIES TO EXPLORE FURTHER

Tapping Into Wellness: Using EFT to Clear Emotional & Physical Pain & Illness, by Kathilyn Solomon

The EFT Manual, by Dawson Church

BOOK FOR EFT AND OTHER ENERGY PRACTITIONERS

How to Be a Great Detective: The Handy-Dandy Guide to Using Kindness, Compassion and Curiosity to Resolve Emotional, Mental & Physical Upsets—For Tappers, Practitioners and Caregivers, by Jondi Whitis

Emotion Code/Body Code

OFFICIAL WEBSITE

www.healerslibrary.com

OFFICIAL BOOK

The Emotion Code, by Dr. Bradley Nelson

Energy Clearing (from Jean Haner)

OFFICIAL WEBSITE

www.jeanhaner.com

OFFICIAL BOOK

Clear Home, Clear Heart: Learn to Clear the Energy of People & Places, by Jean Haner

The Five Elements

WEBSITES

Take a quiz to find out your Five Element personality type:

http://learnthefiveelements.com/

GOOD QUESTIONS AND ANSWERS ABOUT REAL-LIFE RELATIONSHIPS AND HOW THEY RELATE TO THE FIVE ELEMENTS

https://5faces.wordpress.com/the-five-elements-model/

BOOK

The Five Elements: Understand Yourself and Enhance Your Relationships with the Wisdom of the World's Oldest Personality Type System, by Dondi Dahlin

Healing Touch

OFFICIAL WEBSITE
www.healingtouchprogram.com

BOOK
Healing Touch: Enhancing Life Through Energy Therapy, by Diane Wardell, Sue Kagel, and Lisa Anselme

Jin Shin Jyutsu

OFFICIAL WEBSITE
https://www.jsjinc.net/

OVERVIEW BOOK
The Touch of Healing: Energizing the Body, Mind, and Spirit with the Art of Jin Shin Jyutsu, by Alice Burmeister with Tom Monte

Pranic Healing

OFFICIAL WEBSITE
http://pranichealing.com

BOOK
Your Hands Can Heal You: Pranic Healing Energy Remedies to Boost Vitality and Speed Recovery from Common Health Problems, by Master Stephen Co and Dr. Eric Robins with John Merryman

Reiki

WEBSITE
www.reiki.org

BOOKS
Essential Reiki: A Complete Guide to an Ancient Healing Art, by Diane Stein

Reiki: The Healing Touch, by William Lee Rand

The Complete Reiki Book: Basic Introduction and Methods of Natural Application: A Complete Guide for Reiki Practice, by William Lubeck

The Spirit of Reiki: From Tradition to Present Fundamental Lines of Transmission, Original Writings, Mastery, Symbols, Treatments, Reiki as a Spiritual Path in Life, and Much More, by William Lubeck, Frank Arjava Petter, and William Lee Rand

Rubenfeld Synergy Method

OFFICIAL WEBSITE

www.rubenfeldsynergy.com

BOOK

The Listening Hand: Self-Healing Through the Rubenfeld Synergy Method of Talk and Touch, by Ilana Rubenfeld

Shiatsu Massage

FOR TRAINING

www.centerpointmn.com

BOOK

The Book of Shiatsu: A Complete Guide to Using Hand Pressure and Gentle Manipulation to Improve Your Health, Vitality, and Stamina, by Paul Lundberg

Tai Chi and Qigong

WEBSITES

www.tcmworld.org/qigong

www.qigonginstitute.org

BOOKS

The Healing Promise of Qi: Creating Extraordinary Wellness Through Qigong and Tai Chi, by Roger Jahnke and Ken Cohen

The Harvard Medical School Guide to Tai Chi: 12 Weeks to a Healthy Body, Strong Heart & Sharp Mind, by Peter M. Wayne, Ph.D., with Mark L. Fuerst

ThetaHealing®

WEBSITE

www.thetahealing.com

BOOK

Theta Healing: Introducing an Extraordinary Energy Healing Modality, by Vianna Stibal

Energy Medicine
(Eden Energy Medicine from Donna Eden and Dr. David Feinstein)

WEBSITES

https://edenenergymedicine.com

www.innersource.net/em

BOOKS

Energy Medicine: Balancing Your Body's Energies for Optimal Health, Joy, and Vitality, by Donna Eden with Dr. David Feinstein

Energy Medicine for Women: Aligning Your Body's Energies to Boost Your Health and Vitality, by Donna Eden with Dr. David Feinstein

The Energies of Love: Invisible Keys to a Fulfilling Partnership, by Donna Eden and David Feinstein

Thought Field Therapy

GENERAL INFORMATION FROM CREATOR DR. ROGER CALLAHAN

http://tfttapping.com

BOOK

Tapping the Healer Within: Using Thought-Field Therapy to Instantly Conquer Your Fears, Anxieties, and Emotional Distress, by Dr. Roger Callahan with Richard Trubo

Co-Dependents Anonymous

http://coda.org

Co-dependency normally refers to behaviors by people in relationships with others who have an active addiction. I look at this term more broadly as I see many people who energetically take on other people's "stuff" in ways that are debilitating. I have found that when these people attend a twelve-step group like Co-Dependents Anonymous, it helps them establish better relationship boundaries, which also helps their energetic boundaries. These meetings are free and widely available.

ACKNOWLEDGMENTS

In a cynical world, thanking God may seem like a fanciful choice. But living from a Higher Love is more radical than anything else I've ever done. My spiritual journey fuels every aspect of my work and I wouldn't have it any other way. For the air in my lungs, the beating of my heart, every unexpected miracle, and for giving me a High Def, Technicolor life. Thank You.

Enormous gratitude to you, Joel Fotinos. I have no idea what inspired you to take a chance on an "unknown kid." Even though you sort of knew me and I'm certainly no kid! You may not have realized it, but with this opportunity you were making a lifelong dream come true for me. It wasn't lost on me, not at all, not for a moment. I'll be forever honored and thankful.

For my immediate family: Mom, Mike, Rose, Sue, Bob, Steve, Silvia, Anthony, Ashley, Frank, Brittany, Alissa, Natalie, and Catherine. And my greater family at large: Beth, Deana, Jackie, Johnny, Katie, Laurie, Sherry, and so many more. You may not always understand what I'm up to, but love me anyway. And truly appreciate your love and support!

I really wish my dad had been here to see this. Thanks, Dad, for making me strong and showing me the value in speaking the truth.

For Donna Eden, Dr. David Feinstein, Dondi Dahlin, and the entire Innersource and Eden Energy Medicine family. You are among my favorite teachers and have boosted my practice in ways I didn't know were needed. The kindness you've shown me means so much. You've given me a glimpse into what's possible with the magical lives you've created. You are always an inspiration.

For Gary Craig, for creating EFT and giving it to the world so generously. For Dr. Roger Callahan, for starting it all. For CJ Puotinen, my first in-person EFT teacher. For AAMET International (Association for the Advancement of Meridian Energy Techniques). For Gwyneth Moss and the EFT Guild members. For Dawson Church and EFT Universe. For the Ortners and Tapping Solution. For every single tapping expert I've interviewed or who has interviewed me; for every newsletter or book written, classes taught, groups conducted, videos taped, podcasts recorded, summits manned, gatherings created (and, at times, invited me to!), feedback given, debates taken part in . . . so, so, so much thanks. Our content-rich industry has served us all well. We are advancing this work forward, each in our own unique way. Let's keep rolling.

For Jondi Whitis. For seeing in me what I was unable to see in myself. For giving me a chance to grow, rise up, be courageous, and shine in ways I wasn't sure I was capable of. For giving this misfit a place to be a trailblazer. For demonstrating kindness, compassion, and diplomacy, always. For being a most loved friend. For giving me my beloved Spring Energy Event community, whom I also thank, just for them being them. And for all that has spawned from it, including the 9 Dammits of Isle la Motte. I look forward to each time we are together. There is no replacing the joy in like-minded community. It has given back to me more than words can express.

For the other three members of the Four Musketeers: Lucie Monroe, Kelly Roughton, and Beth Sorger. I thought of you all often throughout the writing of this book. You will see your ideas and wisdom sprinkled throughout. Our partnership and friendships have advanced my work in ways I could never have expected. More important, you make me feel at home. You've given me a safe place for questions, ideas, creativity, and vulnerability. You've weathered my complaints and celebrated my successes. I cherish you all.

For friends old and new, who remind me I'm okay just as I am. More people than can possibly be mentioned. Big love to Beth Bachmann, Donniee Barnes, Mary Day Bodenstein, Agnes Brophy, Mary Kay Carney and Diane and family, Chris and Amy Delucca, Elaine DeMars, Pat Dobbs, John Fiore, Celine Fitzpatrick, Dave and Bernalee Garland, Joan Granda, Adrienne Hew and the Hew-Brown family, James Hyler, Dave Korman, Cathy Krupsky, Kevin "Boo" Leavitt, Tina Mannino, Julio "Cage" Martinez, Regina McLoughlin, Chris Medina, Ivette Mendez, Sherri Nicholas, Nicole Nicholson, Alicia North, John O'Neill, Elanna Posner, Véronique Ramsey and the Ramsey family, Scott Raposa, Leslie Robinson, Ann Sheridan, Brian Streeper, Sylvia Taylor, Xan and Greg Yanosh, and Ulana Zahajkewycz.

To my entire Center for Spiritual Living North Jersey family, especially Rev. Michelle Wadleigh, the ministers, Practitioner Core, the amazing musicians, board, staff, members, and volunteers. And to the greater CSL organization along with the Practitioner Council members. You provide loving spaces where all are welcome. You teach people how to fly. See, look what happened to me!

To my tapping partners: Sebastiaan van der Schrier, Yvonne Toeset, Linda Wood, and Erik Zoeteweij. Anything I want to say here will violate confidentiality. Ha! You all mean so much to me. You have created safe spaces where I have opened up, come clean, and healed. You've taught me it's safe to trust. I am loads lighter due to our partnerships.

To my prayer partners, most consistently Toni Hamilton and Harry Pickens. I think this book may be your doing! Thank you for joining me in sacred alliance and holding what's possible.

For every client, student, tapping group participant, and newsletter subscriber I've ever had. Your support of me and this work, the trust and courage you've demonstrated, and your willingness to learn and to heal both thrills and humbles me. Know you are always deeply appreciated.

For Frank Giordano and Dr. Dominic Smorra. You wear the titles of massage therapist and chiropractor respectively. Both of you are true healers who elevate your professions. You have taken such amazing care of me. I trust that all the tension and kinks in my shoulders and back from writing will soon be eased. My body thanks you.

To the staff and students at Vision Loss Alliance of New Jersey, especially Linda Groszew and Elsa Zavoda, I thank you for giving me a place at your table. You prove that organizations and individuals *are* open to the gifts of energy healing. My class is one of the highlights of my week!

INDEX

ABOUT THE AUTHOR

An experienced practitioner with a thriving practice, KRIS FERRARO provides the perfect introduction to energy healing, including quick and easy techniques that anyone can incorporate into their lives. A rich resources section will help readers further explore the world of energy healing and develop their practice. Anyone looking to understand and practice energy healing in their own life should Start Here!